What Happened Next?

Ripple effects of Bible stories

Richard Littledale

Copyright © 2025 Richard Littledale

First published 2025 by Authentic Media Limited,
PO Box 6326, Bletchley, Milton Keynes, MK1 9GG.
authenticmedia.co.uk

The right of Richard Littledale to be identified as the Author of this Work has
been asserted in accordance with the
Copyright, Designs and Patents Act 1988.

All rights reserved.
No part of this publication may be reproduced, stored
in a retrieval system, or transmitted in any form or by any means,
electronic, mechanical, photocopying, recording or otherwise, without
the prior permission of the publisher or a licence permitting restricted copying.
In the UK such licences are issued by the Copyright Licensing Agency, 5th
Floor, Shackleton House, 4 Battle Bridge Lane, London SE1 2HX.

British Library Cataloguing in Publication Data
A catalogue record for this book is available from the British Library.
ISBN: 978-1-78893-367-4
978-1-78893-368-1 (e-book)

Scripture quotations taken from
The Holy Bible, New International Version Anglicised
Copyright © 1979, 1984, 2011 Biblica
Used by permission of Hodder & Stoughton Ltd, an Hachette UK company.
All rights reserved.
'NIV' is a registered trademark of Biblica
UK trademark number 1448790.

Cover design by Fresh Vision Design

Dedication

For Matt and Helen

Because '*What happens next*' is always in God's hands

Contents

Foreword		ix
Chapter 1:	Imagine That!	1
Chapter 2:	How to Use This Book	8
Story 1:	The Boat Next Door	11
Story 2:	The Blacksmith	14
Story 3:	Battle Shy	17
Story 4:	After the Crash	20
Story 5:	Saved by the Sword	23
Story 6:	Second Sight	26
Story 7:	Quiet Ship	29
Story 8:	The Reluctant Vine	32
Story 9:	Not So Grand	35
Story 10:	A Swineherd Speaks Out	38
Story 11:	Prison News	41
Story 12:	The Picnic	44
Story 13:	Unabashed	47
Story 14:	Mr and Mrs Pilate	50
Story 15:	Up and At It	53
Story 16:	The House with a Hole in the Roof	56
Story 17:	The Girl with an Appetite	59
Story 18:	The Homecoming	62

Contents

Story 19:	The Abandoned Cloak	65
Story 20:	An Empty Upper Room	68
Story 21:	The Centurion Who Saw	71
Story 22:	A Lifetime of Shame	74
Story 23:	All the Way Home	77
Story 24:	Mother's Boy	80
Story 25:	After the Perfume	83
Story 26:	The Tale of an Inn (1)	86
Story 27:	The Tale of an Inn (2)	89
Story 28:	Tree House	92
Story 29:	A Sweeper's Tale	95
Story 30:	After the Sacking	98
Story 31:	A Scar to Savour	101
Story 32:	After the Rip	104
Story 33:	After the Banquet	107
Story 34:	Stargazing	110
Story 35:	No Mat Today	113
Story 36:	The Woman and the Sand	116
Story 37:	Fussed and Fuzzy	119
Story 38:	Freed but Not Free	122
Story 39:	A New Family	125
Story 40:	The Tale of a Tomb	128
Story 41:	A Garden Walk	131
Story 42:	A Netful of Fish	134
Story 43:	Onwards and Upwards	137
Story 44:	A Trail of Footprints	140
Story 45:	A Change of Fortune	143

Contents

Story 46:	The Jail Menders	146
Story 47:	Officially Awkward	149
Story 48:	A New Trade	152
Story 49:	The Careless Listener	155
Story 50:	Sandy Knees and Heavy Hearts	158
Story 51:	On the Beach	161
Story 52:	Full Stop	164

What Happens Next?	167
Bibliography	171
End Notes	173

Foreword

I remember when Richard first floated this idea my way. It was over our usual coffee order at our usual table in our usual café of choice. This scene had taken place many times before: the coffees, the setting, the flow of ideas between two 'creative types' who also love to preach. This feverish creative exchange would often happen over coffees slowly going cold from neglect and with no attention paid to the busyness around us. This moment was no different but the idea that landed on my side of the sturdy wooden table certainly was.

Richard explained how he wanted to explore the minor characters, the bit players, the background faces we meet in the Bible and imagine what happened to them following the incredible events and miracles they experienced. My lovely hot cappuccino was doomed to be tepid brown waste as the creative chain reaction began in my mind. We often share our ideas with a certain amount of vulnerability, since to share our creativity is to share something personal with the hope of affirmation from the recipient. My reaction, I'm sure, left no doubt in Richard's mind that this was an idea worth developing. The possibilities it created felt infinite, the creative challenge it posed was exciting and more importantly, it could be a tool to inspire people to read the Bible in a new way – what is more

Foreword

exciting than that? After a flurry of ideas in response and a quick sip of cold coffee, I encouraged him to pursue it. I left that day with a mind that whirred with possibilities; Richard left with the affirmation and encouragement he needed.

What happened next, you may ask? The answer to that requires no imagination because you are holding it in your hands. In this book, Richard has given colour and life to those minor biblical characters who witnessed some of the most incredible moments in human history. These are characters who we may only meet in a few lines or even words but who no less had a part to play in God's narrative.

With a little sprinkling of God-given imagination, we are given the opportunity to see the fuller picture of how these events may have played out in the lives and people that experienced them first-hand. We meet people and characters we may never have paid much attention to before. We may see perspectives on events we have never considered. We may even feel our own imagination being fired as we begin to read Bible stories through a new lens, placing ourselves right in the middle of the miracles and events recorded in Scripture. You may even see a reflection of yourself within this book. Perhaps you will recognise the reactions, emotions and responses. This book will help you develop a biblical imagination that will bring to life the words on the thin pages of your Bible. It will help remind you that within Scripture we meet an eclectic range of people who each have their own perspective on and experience of God, people who may look similar to us.

Foreword

Yet this book is more than that. This book will help the reader remember that the Bible is about real events, real people and a very real God who has been present in the world since it was first shaped by his hands. This collection of imagined stories helps us see that so often God's plan collides with our mortal lives and when that happens, nothing is the same again. Like a powerfully struck cue ball hitting a carefully laid out tapestry of coloured snooker balls, nothing is where it was originally found as the pattern changes on the table, of course all with a plan behind each skilful strike of the cue.

After reading this beautifully written collection of stories, I would encourage you to write one of your own. Only make the answer to the question 'what happened next' about your story and your life after God moved powerfully in it. After all, our testimony and our journey of faith is exactly that; the 'what happened next' after God's plan collided with our life. There is power in that, and your part may feel as small as some of those you will meet in this book. Yet they are no less important to the wonderful and perfect plan God has for each one of us and more broadly, the plan he has for all.

From that first conversation in that café to holding a copy of the finished book in my hand, I am reminded that God's plan is as wonderful as it is mysterious, but we all have our part to play and he delights in that fact. We have to be brave in trusting it and using the gifts he has given us to carry out our part; in this case, the wonderful gift of imagination.

Matthew Gower

Chapter 1

Imagine That!

Warning: this book may fire your imagination

What a very strange way to begin a book! After all, we generally regard the use of the imagination as a good thing. 'Use your imagination!' is employed as a gentle rebuke for those who cannot or will not see beyond the obvious. Whilst writing this book, I paid a visit to the local toy shop to select a birthday gift for my 1-year-old granddaughter, and spent some time browsing the shelves of the 'early years' section. What struck me most (apart from the gorgeous colours and the temptation to buy everything on display) was how much creativity and skill has been invested by toy designers. The toys are specifically designed to encourage the youngest children to *make up their own* worlds and games as they play.

Once at primary school, children are encouraged to pursue their imagination in words and pictures as they begin to develop. The best teachers are the ones who allow the children to paint a pink zebra or describe a spaceship that can jump galaxies in seconds without ever suggesting that such things are impossible. The joy of creativity at this stage should not be stifled by the boundaries of the possible. As the children grow older and enter secondary education, imagination may be invested in writing the best stories or asking the most incisive questions in the science lab. Those who go on to higher education and beyond will be encouraged to harness insight to imagination so as to cross boundaries and find breakthroughs in all kinds of fields. Imagination is the key to innovating the unseen and creating the unmade.

Once into adult life, many of us try to keep that playfulness and imagination alive so as to preserve a hopeful and curious view of the world. Bookshops are full of 'imaginary' stories in the fiction section, and the multi-billion-dollar movie industry plays consciously, and expensively, to our imaginations. The word 'imagineering' was originally coined by the Aluminium Corporation of America to suggest a fusion of imagination and engineering. It was later used by Walt Disney, Inc. (the company responsible for the creation of Disneyland) and registered as a Disney trademark in 1989. Today, *imagineers* are architects, designers, costume-makers, illustrators, engineers and others whose work entertains billions of people at the Disney parks around the world. Walt Disney himself said that 'Disneyland will never be completed as long as there is imagination in the world'.[1] In short, imagination is a good thing.

So, why the warning?

Historically, the Christian church has not always encouraged the use of the imagination, at least not so far as the Scriptures are concerned. To a certain extent, this has been a fear on the part of the clergy about loss of control. If the Scriptures are left to run amok in people's imaginations, then who knows where it might lead? If people use Scripture as a springboard to their imaginations, and this leads to the creation of new theological insights, who is to say which is human and which is divine in the finished product? Some years ago, I was writing a master's dissertation with the not-so-snappy title: 'The Preacher as Translator: A Model for Preaching in the Twenty-first Century'. My research on the topic led me deep into the world of Bible translation, equivalent meaning and the great divide between formal equivalence and dynamic equivalence. Simply put, the former seeks a translation which is as faithful as possible to the *words* of the original text, and the latter seeks a translation which is as close as possible to the *impact* of the original text. The King James Bible would be an example of the former and *The Message* an example of the latter. Whilst many love the immediacy and accessibility of dynamic equivalence translations, others worry about the degree to which the translator's own imagination and supposition has intruded into the process. Here is the church's unease with the upstart imagination writ large.

Church historians might also point to the birth of various heresies in the imagination too. When I was a first-year theology student, I had not really encountered hard-line Calvinism before. However, I soon became aware of it. One of my more Calvinist colleagues passed on with great relish the story of Calvin being asked what God was doing before he created the world. Reputedly, the great man replied that he was 'stoking the fires of hell for those who ask impertinent questions'! The story, however, is not quite what it seems. Calvin had in fact inherited this apocryphal tale from Augustine, and Augustine was unable to pin down its source:

> Behold, I answer to him who asks, What was God doing before He made heaven and earth? I answer not, as a certain person is reported to have done facetiously (avoiding the pressure of the question), He was preparing hell, says he, for those who pry into mysteries.[2]

Could it be that this is an imaginary tale about the dangers of the imagination, maybe?

Imagination may be alright outside the church in theatre, literature and cinema, but what about if it crosses the threshold of the church? It is interesting to note that the earliest forms of ecclesiastical theatre took place outside the church, often on specially erected platforms. Once they came inside, they brought the danger of imagination with them. The threat has always been not so much the imagination itself as its impudence. A high regard for the authenticity and inspiration of Scripture makes us wary of anything which appears to embellish it or add to its story. The fear is two-fold, namely arrogance and subversion. We fear an arrogance that gives us licence to alter Scripture, and a subversion that undermines its power. When I wrote my handbook on narrative preaching in 2007, I had to allay precisely those fears. Consider this, for example, on 'first voice' narrative preaching:

> To speak on behalf of another person is always difficult. However, to do it on behalf of a dead Biblical character who cannot be consulted, and whose story we regard as part of the inspired word of God is even more risky![3]

One of my great champions when researching that book and since has been Thomas Troeger. In his book *Imagining a Sermon* he speculates as to whether preachers, in particular, dismiss imagination whilst secretly envying its powers. He then goes on to chart the church's changing relationship with the imagination as it gradually drains away in the pre-Enlightenment era, and is banished by the Reformation, only to reappear once more after the Enlightenment. The book is playful at times, pointing out, for instance, that it takes 'imagination to imagine a world without imagination'.[4] Overall, he suggests that finite minds are incapable of grappling with the infinite breadth and depth and height of God without harnessing the imagination. I could not agree more.

As a person who now consumes sermons more than preaching them, I am desperate for the preacher to capture my imagination. Until my dying day I shall always need to be *taught* as a Christian, but I also need to be encouraged, enlivened, challenged and inspired. The left brain with its focus on analytical thought and the right brain with its inclination towards imagination and story both need to be stimulated. Furthermore, the more neural pathways we forge between the two, the more of what we hear is likely to be retained. Sundays tend to find me now in the pew, rather than the pulpit, and I am unbelievably grateful to those preachers who have gone the extra mile in harnessing their imagination as a means to reach mine.

It is in the hope of harnessing yours that I offer these fifty-two stories to you.

What Happened Next?

What they are not

Let me be clear that the stories you read in the following pages are not Scripture. They make no claim to the spiritual depth or divine authority which sits on those pages. Nor are they factual. Since I was not there after the feeding of the 5,000, nor when the ripped temple curtain was brought into the workshops for repair, I cannot give an account of what *actually* happened. On many occasions I have 'invented' an eyewitness to these events, so that they can tell us about them with all the immediacy of a person who was actually there. If, when I get to heaven it turns out some of the people are just as described, I hope I can shake their hand and ask them for the full story. The other thing to note is that each of these stories is just one possible version of what happened next. We shall talk about some of the other versions a little later on. Before we are done, I shall encourage you to go away and find your own alternative versions.

What they are

Matthew Gower is a friend of mine, who I have been mentoring as he explores a call to ministry. When he first heard an audio version of these stories, he talked about 'the story of Jesus colliding with the stories of individuals', and that is a good summary of how these stories work. Each reflects on what happens when the lives of different people collide with the plans and activities of God. Some are amazed, some are terrified, some are puzzled and none are left unchanged. These stories show us how those aftershocks may have unfolded, though we cannot know for certain, of course.

The Bible can be read as one vast narrative, stretching like an arc over all human history from the first moment of creation to the final 'amen' spoken in the New Jerusalem. Beneath that arc are kings and beggars, shepherds and prostitutes, fishermen and jailers. Most of them can occupy only a few sentences of that bigger story, and so we never get to see the marks left on their lives by playing their part. Consider these stories as a telephoto lens, zooming in on the faces of those involved, with all their tears and smiles.

Of course, you may find I have described these people in exactly the way that you do *not* imagine them. Often this happens when a movie producer brings one of your favourite stories to life, and you find that the characters look nothing like the way you have always pictured them. If so, then my prayer is that this would bring you right back to those original stories in the Bible so that you can exercise your own imagination on how the characters in them would have looked or sounded or felt. In this way, the fifty-two stories serve as a catalyst to further, deeper reading of Scripture and an ongoing habit of interpretation. If this book reawakens a love of the Bible's stories, and sends us back to its pages with eyes and ears wide open, then it will have done its job.

Chapter 2

How to Use This Book

The fact that this book contains fifty-two devotions *may* mean that you choose to read one each week throughout the year. They are presented here in the order in which the original stories appear in the Bible. Read that way, they will take you from Genesis to Revelation in the course of one year. Then again, you may find that you get caught up in these little stories and decide to consume them over a shorter period. However you do it, the guidelines below will help you to make the most of them.

Bible passage

Always start with the Bible passage printed at the top of the page. The verses quoted give you just enough context to make sense of the story which follows. However, if you have time and access to a Bible, then reading a little more of the Bible story will always pay dividends.

First reading

These stories are intentionally short, just enough to pique your imagination. On the first reading, simply go through and get a sense of what is happening.

How to Use This Book

Pause

A pause in reading functions a bit like the white space around the edge of this page – allowing you to focus on what matters. Take a few moments to allow the story to 'soak into' your imagination.

Second reading

This time, read the story whilst actively engaging your senses. If you had been there when the story unfolded, what might you have seen or heard? With some of them, there may have been particular tastes or smells too. Do everything you can to 'inhabit' the story as you read it. This means that your reading will take you a little longer, but you may find yourself savouring the story more that way.

● ● ● **Pause to reflect**

This is a slightly more intentional pause than the previous one, and will give you a nudge to reflect on something you have seen in the story, or to consider how you might have behaved if you had been there at the time.

What Happened Next?

Prayer

Use the written prayer as a springboard for your own.

● ● ● **Act on it!**

This will suggest something that you might do by way of a response to what you have read.

Story 1

The Boat Next Door

> Noah was six hundred years old when the floodwaters came on the earth. And Noah and his sons and his wife and his sons' wives entered the ark to escape the waters of the flood. Pairs of clean and unclean animals, of birds and of all creatures that move along the ground, male and female, came to Noah and entered the ark, as God had commanded Noah. And after the seven days the floodwaters came on the earth.
>
> *(Gen. 7:6–10)*

Despite the rain, for most of them this was the most peaceful day they could remember for a long time. It had begun with Noah clearing every tree and bush from his land and ploughing it flat, as if to make a workspace. After that had come the timber – wagon after wagon after wagon of it for days on end. From sunrise to sunset they would come, and the background music to every conversation had become the rattle of the wheels, the rumble as the logs were released, and then the crash as they fell to the ground.

After that, conversation had become almost impossible, with the sound of sawing and hammering drowning out all else. As if the sound wasn't bad enough, there was the light. As Noah's monstrous construction rose into the air, all their houses began to fall under its shadow. People found excuses to stay away from home for longer and longer, as they did not wish to look out on its high sides and ridiculous length.

What Happened Next?

Then, when at last the saws and hammers fell silent, another noise started up in the far distance. At first, it sounded like a roll of distant thunder. When it got nearer, though, more experienced ears said it sounded like a stampede – the clatter of hundreds of hooves all churning up the ground in unison. It turned out not just to be hooves, but paws, claws and feet of every kind. This past week there had been animals passing by that they had never seen in their entire lives. When the last of them entered the monstrous boat, a kind of grateful hush fell over the quagmire which they had churned up.

The last sound was the creaking of ropes as Noah and his sons heaved and tugged to draw up the boat's enormous gangplank. It fell shut with an almighty crash which seemed to rock the earth itself. After that, the rain began to fall – at first in a gentle patter and then in the steady drumbeat of a real downpour. Gratefully, Noah's neighbours turned away from the spectacle and snuggled down to sit it out. 'Safe as houses' was the phrase which came to mind.

● ● ● Pause to reflect

I fear that whenever I read the story of Noah I am inclined to smirk at his neighbours, as if I could never possibly behave that way. I wonder if that is true, though? If God tells a friend or neighbour or loved-one to do something which we regard as strange, do we accept it or reject it?

Prayer

Dear God, sometimes I wonder how I would have reacted if I had been one of Noah's neighbours. I know that so often I fail to notice what you are really up to. Please make me better at it today, I pray. Amen.

● ● ● Act on it!

If you know someone who is making a life-change in response to God's guidance, ask them about it, and then offer to pray with them, or for them.

Story 2

The Blacksmith

> Then the LORD said to Moses, 'Stretch out your hand over the sea so that the waters may flow back over the Egyptians and their chariots and horsemen.' Moses stretched out his hand over the sea, and at daybreak the sea went back to its place. The Egyptians were fleeing towards it, and the LORD swept them into the sea. The water flowed back and covered the chariots and horsemen – the entire army of Pharaoh that had followed the Israelites into the sea. Not one of them survived.
>
> *(Exod. 14:26–28)*

There used to be a blacksmith on the eastern shore of the Red Sea, far up towards the north. I don't know if it is still there but ask anyone about 'the blacksmith with the sign' and they will soon tell you all about it. The sign outside was not a horseshoe or anything like it – but a sort of sculpture. At its base were two chariot wheels fused together, flanked by two spears. If you knew what you were looking for, you could see that the spears were Egyptian-made, fine craftsmanship with a cartouche of hieroglyphs on the shaft. There were spots of rust, as if they had spent time under water, and one of the chariot wheels was buckled and twisted, as if it had been in some terrible accident.

I went in and asked about it one day, and the blacksmith looked up from his anvil and called for his father to come through from the back room. He was delighted to be asked,

The Blacksmith

and there was an orange-red twinkle in his eye from the flames of the forge. Seeing how interested I was, he took me down the road to see his own father in the tiny family home. Between bouts of coughing, he told me all about the terrible, wonderful day they had crossed the Red Sea, and how they had escaped onto dry land. He was one of the brave ones who had looked back, just in time to see the mighty army of Pharaoh swept away like children's toys in the angry flood as the waters came rushing back. For days afterwards, he told me, people scavenged along the waters for the objects they could find.

'That's where the sign came from,' he said, with a hint of pride. He went on to tell me about donkey carts with fine Egyptian chariot wheels that plied their trade in the villages. Somewhere there was a weathervane made from swords and at least one farmer had lashed a few spears together to make a seed drill for his farm. 'Nice of them to help us out,' he said. 'After all, they owed us.'

It is many years since I went there now, but that day is ever with me. Every time I hear the word 'ploughshare' I think of a certain farmer with his 'recycled' plough and I smile.

● ● ● **Pause to reflect**

Very often we interpret answered prayers in a very one-dimensional way, as if the only thing which matters is what happened to me. A single act by God may answer the different prayers of many people.

Prayer

Dear God, sometimes it is easy to forget the great things you have done. They pass by in a flash, and we move onto the next thing. Today, I ask that you would help me to remember some of the wonderful things you have done in my life. Amen.

● ● ● Act on it!

Choose a prayer which you know to have been answered and hold it up to the light to see how many people gained from it in different ways.

Story 3

Battle Shy

> The LORD said to Gideon, 'You have too many men. I cannot deliver Midian into their hands, or Israel would boast against me, "My own strength has saved me." Now announce to the army, "Anyone who trembles with fear may turn back and leave Mount Gilead."' So twenty-two thousand men left, while ten thousand remained.
>
> *(Judg. 7:2-3)*

To live on this road near the Eastern border had not been a good thing, not for a long time. This was the route which the raiders took, every single time. On the way in they would be merciless, like locusts destroying everything in their wake. On the way out, they would be drunk with success and keen to vent their bloodlust on anyone, young or old, who dared to show their face. In fact, we had learned not to. All who lived along that road had learned to make ourselves all but invisible – using trees and bushes, straw piles and earth banks for cover.

On that bright morning, we were astonished that the sound was coming from the 'other' direction. Hundreds and then thousands of men were marching *towards* the border to take the fight to our enemies. As this dawned on us, so we came out from hiding, apparently seeping from every nook and cranny. Wave after wave after wave of them came marching by and our very hearts swelled with pride.

What Happened Next?

Some clapped and cheered, whilst others bit a bottom lip and shook their heads as if they could not believe their eyes. Maybe this would be the end for our greedy and bloodthirsty neighbours across the border? It took many hours for them to pass by, and when they had, the head man nodded sagely and said that 32,000 fighting men had passed through our village that day. Of course, no one had a mind to argue, and all afternoon into the evening people sat around their fires or talked in the street of the dramatic victory which would surely follow. Would we hear the sound of the fighting from across the border, we wondered? Would we hear the clash of steel upon steel, or at least the enormous victory cry when battle was done? That night, we slept soundly in our beds, sure that all would be well.

In the morning, the footsteps were back – but this time they were heading home again. Not a single one of them bore the scars of battle, and not a single one was smiling, either. Whatever had happened? That same head man sadly counted 22,000 men that day, and there would be another 9,000 and more before the sun went down. How ever could a battle be won with so few left to fight it?

● ● ● **Pause to reflect**

Often the gap between elation and dejection can be no longer than a heartbeat. When things appear to be going wrong, we sometimes need to take a longer view which takes account of God's longer plan.

Prayer

Dear God, when it seems like the odds are impossibly stacked against your children, help me to remember that you delight in doing the impossible. Today, I remember especially those of your children who feel overwhelmed by circumstance or outnumbered by the forces ranged against them. Stand with them, I pray. Amen.

● ● ● Act on it!

If you have any prayer letters to hand, pick out the one request which seems most impossible, and make a point of praying for that one. In the absence of prayer letters, visit the website of any mission agency and look at their latest list of prayer requests.

Story 4

After the Crash

Samson said, 'Let me die with the Philistines!' Then he pushed with all his might, and down came the temple on the rulers and all the people in it. Thus he killed many more when he died than while he lived. Then his brothers and his father's whole family went down to get him. They brought him back and buried him between Zorah and Eshtaol in the tomb of Manoah his father. He had led Israel twenty years.

(Judg. 16:30-31)

Today had been a noisy day for those in the shadow of the temple. At first there had been the trumpets from the walls at dawn's first light to announce that this would be a day of feasting and revelry. After that had come the feet – shuffling, walking, running and marching. With them they brought that curious multiple sound which accompanies any crowd – somewhere between a hum and a babble. There were children squealing with delight, mothers calling after them, traders calling out to sell their wares, and the occasional bark of an order from the soldiers trying to keep them all in check.

Once assembled in the temple, or crowded onto the roof, there had been all sorts of music and pageantry. When the roar of the mob went up a notch, the crowd beyond the stadium gathered that Samson was coming. Once the scourge of all his enemies, he was now the poor blind plaything of the king. Apparently, he was still an entertaining spectacle, though.

Just as the roar of the crowd reached fever pitch, it was replaced with the sounds of thousands screaming as the walls and then the roof came crashing down. The rumble seemed to go on and on, long after the biggest pieces of masonry had fallen and was replaced by a fading symphony of cries for help, which grew weaker and weaker as the day wore on. In the end, like the cloud of dust which had erupted at the time, even the sound seemed to nestle itself back among the broken stones and all was quiet.

Just before dusk, a little family group came down the road, pulling a flat cart between them. They stopped at the edge of the rubble and clambered up the mound towards the centre. After that they worked and worked until their hands bled, scrabbling their way down through the rubble. At last, they found their prize and carefully loaded the body of a great mountain of a man onto their cart. As they wheeled him past me, I noticed that his head had clearly been roughly shaven – but here and there his hair and beard were growing, as if fighting back.

● ● ● Pause to reflect

The fact that we have made foolish decisions along the way, as Samson had, does not mean that our path is set for life. With God, change is always possible.

What Happened Next?

Prayer

Dear God, today I pray for those who are nearing the end of their days, for whatever reason. May you hear their prayer, be it ever so quiet, even as you heard Samson's. Please enable them to give glory to you, even at the last, I pray. Amen.

● ● ● **Act on it!**

After reflecting on this ending story, why not find the location of your nearest hospice and take a card or a small gift in for the staff, to thank them for making the end as good as it can be for all their patients?

Story 5

Saved by the Sword

> The king said, 'This one says, "My son is alive, and your son is dead," while that one says, "No! Your son is dead and mine is alive."' Then the king said, 'Bring me a sword.' So, they brought a sword for the king. He then gave an order: 'Cut the living child in two and give half to one and half to the other.' The woman whose son was alive was deeply moved out of love for her son and said to the king, 'Please, my lord, give her the living baby! Don't kill him!' But the other said, 'Neither I nor you shall have him. Cut him in two!' Then the king gave his ruling: 'Give the living baby to the first woman. Do not kill him; she is his mother.'
>
> *(1 Kgs 3:23-27)*

Always when the king had spoken, all other voices fell silent, and eyes were turned respectfully to the floor. The two women, along with all the courtiers, bowed their heads as if receiving the king's words like a priestly blessing. There would be no comeback or argument. There never was. Instead of handing the sword to the servant who had brought it in, the king stood and let it clatter to floor. The sound of metal on the flagstones sounded deafening in that big space. Slowly and deliberately, he brushed between the two women, refusing to look them in the eye. He had seen enough of those faces and heard enough of those voices for one day. He stopped and turned, though, at the sound of the child as it gurgled and then started to cry. Cupping a callused hand behind the infant's head, he looked the child in the face and hushed him. 'Maybe you'll come back here one day,' he said, and then swept from the room with courtiers in attendance.

The child's mother held him tightly and made her way towards the exit. All the way, her eyes were on him, or on the floor – nowhere else. Suddenly this private love of mother for child felt far too public and she wanted to be away from everyone. A few moments later the other woman followed too. All the fight and anger were gone, to be replaced by the crushing ache of losing her child. Before sunset tonight, whilst the king feasted and the other woman nursed her son, she would attend a burial and watch as her little crumpled son was lowered away from her sight.

Beyond the palace door where the king had disappeared, she looked to the God who had put him on the throne. Biting her lip, and wiping away a tear which now rolled unbidden down her cheek, she wondered bitterly whether *he* would ever know how it felt to lose a child.

● ● ● Pause to reflect

We regard this story, quite rightly, as one of great wisdom. However, it is also a story of terrible loss. The ability to see the less than obvious side to any story is one for which we should pray often, lest we make hasty judgements.

Prayer

Dear God, I am unbelievably grateful today that you chose to lose your own child for my sake. Thank you for your limitless love, and may you be especially close today to those who mourn the loss of a child. Amen.

● ● ● Act on it!

Why not make a donation to a charity which deals with neo-natal and infant child loss? For example, see Sands – www.sands.org.uk

Story 6

Second Sight

> As the enemy came down towards him, Elisha prayed to the LORD, 'Strike this army with blindness.' So, he struck them with blindness, as Elisha had asked. Elisha told them, 'This is not the road and this is not the city. Follow me, and I will lead you to the man you are looking for.' And he led them to Samaria. After they entered the city, Elisha said, 'LORD, open the eyes of these men so they can see.' Then the LORD opened their eyes and they looked, and there they were, inside Samaria. When the king of Israel saw them, he asked Elisha, 'Shall I kill them, my father? Shall I kill them?' 'Do not kill them,' he answered. 'Would you kill those you have captured with your own sword or bow? Set food and water before them so that they may eat and drink and then go back to their master.'
>
> *(2 Kgs 6:18–22)*

Like many cities, this one has places to eat and drink just inside the city gate. Many a traveller, after making their way along dusty roads in the blazing sun, wants nothing more than a cup of cool drink before they take another step into the city. Take a careful look, though, and you will find that this one is a little unusual.

The sign which bears the name of the tavern hangs from a twisted sword. More precisely, it is an Aramean sword. The herbs by the door grow now inside an upturned Aramean helmet. Sometimes, as his party trick, the landlord will bring out four, five or six drinks balanced on a broad Aramean sword.

Second Sight

These things are not the spoils of war, though. These things were left by the men who once ate and drank here. Not only that, but instead of sneaking them away out of sight of their commanders, it was those very commanders who told them to leave them behind. A city who had spared their lives and treated them as guests deserved some reward for their kindness, they reckoned. They had arrived here as blind and helpless as new-born kittens, unable to see, much less to fight. It was when the man of God left that one after another began to rub their eyes and savour the power of sight once more. Gasps of surprise turned to shouts of relief and even to laughter before the feasting began.

Of course, many of the valuable items were sold by those who snatched them up, as you might expect. In the main, it was those who served the Aramean soldiers that day who kept their souvenirs. To them, the reminder that God's enemies were just men fighting the wrong enemy was worth more than any gold.

● ● ● Pause to reflect

So often we understand an armed conflict as having a 'right' and a 'wrong' side to it. However, there will be reluctant participants on both sides, and all pay a heavy price.

What Happened Next?

Prayer

Dear God, what a wonderful surprise those soldiers had when blindness turned to light and fighting to feasting. Today I thank you for the many times you have taken me by surprise with your unexpected blessings. Amen.

● ● ● **Act on it!**

Find a world map today and locate the place where one of the world's armed conflicts is happening. Now rest your fingers lightly on that place as you pray for all whose lives are affected by the fighting.

Story 7

Quiet Ship

> The sea was getting rougher and rougher. So, they asked him, 'What should we do to you to make the sea calm down for us?' 'Pick me up and throw me into the sea,' he replied, 'and it will become calm. I know that it is my fault that this great storm has come upon you.' Instead, the men did their best to row back to land. But they could not, for the sea grew even wilder than before. Then they cried out to the LORD, 'Please, LORD, do not let us die for taking this man's life. Do not hold us accountable for killing an innocent man, for you, LORD, have done as you pleased.' Then they took Jonah and threw him overboard, and the raging sea grew calm.
> *(Jonah 1:11–15)*

With an unseemly splosh, their ragged passenger disappeared into the angry, broiling sea, which instantly swallowed him. For so many hours the wind had howled around the ship and beaten a tattoo of ropes on timber that at first nobody noticed it had fallen silent. Their backs and shoulders were so stiff from pulling with all their might against the enormous waves that nobody saw the sea was now flat. The only sound was the reassuring creak of the mast and the slight slap of gentle waves on the hull.

Embarrassed, they moved away from the stern where they had stood not a moment before, swinging that helpless man between them, before flinging him as far from their endangered boat as possible. It was a terrible thing to do, a defiance of the sea's laws and their own humanity, but they

What Happened Next?

had seen no alternative. Nobody would meet another man's eyes – instead, looking up at the clearing sky or out at the flat surface of the sea. Maybe they hoped he would somehow rise and wave them off? Maybe they feared that he would surface just long enough to point an accusing finger at them before disappearing forever? Neither happened, and the sea yielded no more sight of him.

After so many hours of the crashing and howling from the storm, at first nobody noticed the silence. Once ashore, none of them would speak of this to their children, or even to each other.

Eventually they moved away and found things with which to busy themselves. One tidied up the ropes that had torn lose in the gale. Another gathered shards of the amphorae that had broken free in the hold and smashed. Two of them made efforts to sweep the remaining water off the deck, and another shipped the oars, since they were no longer needed. When at last the remains of the sail ran up the mast and they pointed the bow once more for Tarshish, in their minds was only one question: Who was this man's God, that he could silence the raging storm in an instant?

● ● ● Pause to reflect

In the whole story of Jonah, there is no one who shows more bravery than these sailors when they refuse his initial instruction to throw him into the sea and try instead to row for the shore. So far as we know, they had no belief in God, and yet their true humanity shows through.

Prayer

Dear God, thank you that Jonah's story was not over at this point, and that so often you can turn bad to good. Today I ask you to draw near to those whose consciences nag them night and day, and who can find no peace. Amen.

● ● ● Act on it!

Have a look through your house to find some piece of equipment or furniture which was made overseas. The chances are that there were merchant sailors who helped to bring it to your door. Why not pray for them today, facing the challenges of life on the high seas?

Story 8

The Reluctant Vine

Jonah had gone out and sat down at a place east of the city. There he made himself a shelter, sat in its shade and waited to see what would happen to the city. Then the LORD God provided a leafy plant and made it grow up over Jonah to give shade for his head to ease his discomfort, and Jonah was very happy about the plant. But at dawn the next day God provided a worm, which chewed the plant so that it withered. When the sun rose, God provided a scorching east wind, and the sun blazed on Jonah's head so that he grew faint. He wanted to die, and said, 'It would be better for me to die than to live.' But God said to Jonah, 'Is it right for you to be angry about the plant?' 'It is,' he said. 'And I'm so angry I wish I were dead.'

(Jonah 4:5–9)

Not many people move to Nineveh. You are either born there or you trade there for a time – but few move there to take up residence. In truth, the old man who lives on the hill to the east of the city cannot really be said to *live* there. He's an odd-looking character, hair and skin bleached as if by something other than the sun, and nose permanently wrinkled as if smelling a vile odour which no one else can detect. He visited the city once and has vowed never to visit it again. Occasionally you catch him staring far out to the west, as if hoping to catch a glimpse of the distant sparkling ocean. He has vowed never to go *there* again, either.

The Reluctant Vine

Instead, he lives here, on the brow of this hill, in a hut cobbled together from the branches and scraps he could find at the side of the road. When not glowering at the city or staring moodily out towards the sea, he works and works at this stubborn little patch of ground to try to make something grow. Everyone who stops by and watches his bent back and flailing arms shakes their heads because they know that this particular soil will yield nothing. The braver ones tell him that and get short shrift for their troubles. Often, he sits them down (without offering them a drink) and tells them how almighty God once made a vine so tall it towered above his head grow here in just one night. If they ask where it is now, he curses, stamps as hard as he can on the ground, mutters something about worms, and turns back to his feverish digging.

All the same, he never starves. There are people in this city who recall his first visit. They tell of him appearing through the city gates like some spectre washed up from the ocean's depths and making his way from street to street with a dire warning for all to heed. They did, judgement did not fall, and the city breathed again. Those who remember all this bring him little baskets of food from time to time. They neither expect nor receive thanks – but he eats it all the same. He tears hungrily at the bread and consumes the fruit – always keeping the pips, every single time. There must be hundreds of them in that soil, but not a single one has grown; or at least not yet.

What Happened Next?

● ● ● **Pause to reflect**

By any scale, Jonah was an incredibly successful preacher, with an entire city responding to his message in repentance and faith. This being so, why do you think he ends up so ill-tempered in the final chapter of the book which bears his name?

Prayer

Dear God, help me to accept your view on things, no matter how unpalatable it might seem. I ask you, too, that you might replace the grumps with grace whenever they come knocking. Amen.

● ● ● **Act on it!**

Try your best to embrace God's surprising perspective today, even when it is a long way from your own.

Story 9

Not So Grand

> On coming to the house, they saw the child with his mother Mary, and they bowed down and worshipped him. Then they opened their treasures and presented him with gifts of gold, frankincense and myrrh. And having been warned in a dream not to go back to Herod, they returned to their country by another route.
>
> *(Matt. 2:11–12)*

On that particular morning, there was an electricity in the air in that particular area of Babylon. There was a frisson of excitement about the place as if something unprecedented were unfolding. There was a good reason for that.

Coming down the road were merchants, tradesmen and even a beggar boy carrying beautiful things. Striding past, as if already calculating what he might make from its sale, a stallholder from the bazaar held a beautiful sword aloft, turning it this way and that to see how it glinted in the sun. Behind him came a whiskery old beggar, usually sat cross-legged on the street corner. Now he strode past with a finely embroidered cloak draped about his shoulders, its tasselled hem brushing the dusty road, as it was a touch too long for him. His head was held high, his chin jutting out, as if he were practising for the role of a nobleman in a play. Next came a trader pushing a flat wooden cart piled high with maps and charts, all pinned down by a highly polished telescope.

What Happened Next?

Around the next corner was the reason for it all. One of the city's wise men, or Magi, had returned from many months travelling in the west, and now he was a changed man. He had arrived home the previous night, dusty and weary from his travels. Nonetheless, at first light he had opened the outer door to the street and started to heap his possessions there for all to take.

As he gleefully handed out his belongings, he declared that the trappings of a wise man no longer suited him. 'I've met a king,' he said. 'An infant king.' He went on to explain that this little king had 'more wisdom in his little finger than I have lodged in my head in a lifetime'. Somehow, his learning didn't seem to matter much any more. He was shedding every trapping of his former life like a snake sheds its skin.

As evening fell, and the light began to fade, he handed over the last things, and headed happily indoors. The one thing he would not give away was his camel and all his travelling clothes. Within a month, he was saddled up and headed west in pursuit of a new master to serve . . .

● ● ● **Pause to reflect**

The Magi are beloved characters in any depiction of Christmas, with their exotic costumes and their exquisite gifts. It is worth remembering that their quest to find Jesus and their decision to worship him would have made them at least oddities and perhaps outcasts on their return home.

Prayer

Dear God, to change our minds is often a hard thing, especially when it involves swallowing our pride. Whenever the time comes for me to do it, give me a hefty measure of your grace, I pray. Amen.

● ● ● **Act on it!**

For this wise man, an encounter with Jesus made him let go of his fine possessions as they did not seem to matter any more. Ask God if there is anything you should be giving away.

Story 10

A Swineherd Speaks Out

> The demons begged Jesus, 'If you drive us out, send us into the herd of pigs.' He said to them, 'Go!' So, they came out and went into the pigs, and the whole herd rushed down the steep bank into the lake and died in the water. Those tending the pigs ran off, went into the town and reported all this, including what had happened to the demon-possessed men. Then the whole town went out to meet Jesus. And when they saw him, they pleaded with him to leave their region.
>
> *(Matt. 8:31–34)*

I know what you are thinking. To be honest, I know what you are smelling too. You wouldn't be the first to say that I smell of them. I don't know whether it's true or not – how should I know? Live with those creatures for enough years and the smell passes you by. There were plenty of people back then who felt like it was a filthy way to earn a living. Maybe I always knew it would come to an end one day – just never in the way it did. To think that a lifetime can change in a single moment amazes me still today.

I earn my living differently now. I own a boat, of all things! Each day, I ferry people out to the spot where it all happened. When we get there, I ship the oars and a kind of quietness settles, boat creaking and waves lapping. They all look at me expectantly, wanting to hear the tale again, even though I have told it a hundred times or more.

I talk about the quiet voice of Jesus and the grotesque, squealing thunder of the stampede. I talk about the smile on that dear madman's face and the scowl on the faces of the villagers. If you ask me, they are more trapped now than that poor man ever was, despite the chains he wore. When you've made a name for yourselves by sending the Messiah away with a flea in his ear, what else have you got?

Story over, they do it every time – peering over the side of the boat as if to see the ghostly faces of the departed swine staring back at them. Occasionally they will look up and turn their gaze to the shore where Jesus was standing when it happened. He's long gone now, of course. Rumour has it that he went in the end to Jerusalem, and then on to other, higher places. The strange thing is that wherever he is, I feel he is with me. How can that be?

● ● ● Pause to reflect

Whilst the madman is the obvious subject of this story, many other people were affected on that day. Whenever a person's life is touched by Christ, it affects all the people in their orbit.

Prayer

Dear God, I thank you for those moments when you have intervened in my life's story and changed everything. It is because of those moments that my life is entirely different today to the way it might have been. On the days when it seems like nothing will ever change, help me to remember them, I pray. Amen.

● ● ● Act on it!

Who is the most recent person you can think of to have come to Christ? How might this have affected their relationships with family, friends and colleagues? Resolve to contact that new Christian today and offer your encouragement.

Story 11

Prison News

When John, who was in prison, heard about the deeds of the Messiah, he sent his disciples to ask him, 'Are you the one who is to come, or should we expect someone else?' Jesus replied, 'Go back and report to John what you hear and see: the blind receive sight, the lame walk, those who have leprosy are cleansed, the deaf hear, the dead are raised, and the good news is proclaimed to the poor.

(Matt. 11:2–5)

All morning they had been lingering on the edge of this crowd, laughing at the stories, gasping at the miracles, and nodding at the words of wisdom. It had been fun to follow the crowd from town to town as they marvelled at the words and touch of Jesus. Occasionally, though, they would exchange nervous glances as if *someone* needed to say *something*. Not one of them could find the right words, and nobody wanted to sour the mood with a tough question. In the end, nobody needed to make the first move, as Jesus took them to one side and asked them gently what was wrong. At that point, the message all came tumbling out, word for word just as John had given it. With an expansive sweep of his arm, Jesus gave them his answer, and this time when the crowd moved on, they stayed behind.

As soon as the crowd had disappeared round the next bend, they looked at one another, nodded, and agreed that they should make their way to see John without delay. Knowing him as they did, they knew that he would have been awaiting their reply as eagerly as a thirsty man longed for water. When at last they reached the city, and then made their way to the fortress, there was the usual interminable delay whilst each guard checked with his superior and so on up the chain that they should be allowed access to their rabbi.

Edging into the cell, they saw that his tired old head was drooping more than ever. This spiritual giant of a man looked overwhelmed now, as if the drab and windowless walls had somehow shrunk him. The fire which once had come with every breath was more of an ember now, but it was still there. 'Well?' he asked, eyes shining momentarily with anticipation. The three of them looked at each other, as if unwilling to speak up. In the end, they all blurted out the words of Jesus at the same moment, and then felt embarrassed, as if they had spoken out of turn. There was silence now, as they awaited his reaction. Would their words be enough? Would he find one last surge of energy and leap to his feet, punching the air in triumph? In the end, there was a barely perceptible nod of his head, and as a tear tracked down the dust of each cheek, he uttered three solemn words.

'I knew it.'

● ● ● Pause to reflect

At times John the Baptist is a firebrand, seeming altogether fearless. At this moment, he is acutely vulnerable, and maybe more accessible to us because of it.

Prayer

Dear God, help me to take a good look at what you are up to today, and to strengthen my faith as a result. I pray in particular for those whose circumstances have made them lose sight of you. Amen.

● ● ● Act on it!

Doubt is something we rarely associate with Christian leaders in the public eye, and yet it is surely there from time to time. Do some internet research. Which Christian leader could you pray for today?

Story 12

The Picnic

'Bring them here to me,' he said. And he told the people to sit down on the grass. Taking the five loaves and the two fish and looking up to heaven, he gave thanks and broke the loaves. Then he gave them to the disciples, and the disciples gave them to the people. They all ate and were satisfied, and the disciples picked up twelve basketfuls of broken pieces that were left over. The number of those who ate was about five thousand men, besides women and children.

(Matt. 14:18–21)

It was just a small village, so news travelled fast. On this occasion, it didn't need to, though – since the news was everywhere at once. If you had walked into the village that night, it was the smell which would have struck you first – smoking fish, broiling fish, steaming fish and everything in between. After that, you would have heard the sound, as if every household had decided to hold a street party on the spur of the moment. There were children squealing with glee as they ran from house to house, and occasional eruptions of laughter as old men told jokes shared a hundred times before which somehow seemed funnier tonight. The tables were full, even as the evening wore on, and nobody seemed in a mood to leave the pool of lamplight around each one and head indoors.

Of course, you could not have stood and watched for long. One and then another and another still would have called you over, shuffled up to make space for the stranger, and plied

The Picnic

you with bread and fish. Households would have vied to offer you their recipe, hoping that their particular herbs would please you the most, but happy just that you were joining in. Soon, between mouthfuls, you would have asked what this was all about, and the conversation would have quietly ebbed away as every head turned to the village elder.

Putting down his bread and simple cup of rough country wine, he would have explained about the blessing on their doorsteps. As evening had fallen, and a crowd who had been listening to Jesus up on the hill had passed through on their way home and ebbed away through the village streets, it had begun. It had started with the poorest families in the village, those who were not expecting to eat tonight; and then spread to others too. People would look out through their doors to see the crowd as it left, only to find a gift at their feet. Little cries had gone up from this street and that as people had found a basket of bread and fish at their doors. The fish was glistening and fresh, and the bread so new as if it had just been baked. 'And that,' he would say, before picking up his cup again, 'is how the party began. Dig in.'

● ● ● Pause to reflect

An element of this story on which we rarely reflect is the original 'donation' of the food. Somebody had to give away the only food they had before the miracle could happen.

What Happened Next?

Prayer

Dear God, sometimes I am so busy questioning what you are up to that I forget to enjoy it. Please help me not to do that today, I pray. Instead, I ask that I might simply savour your blessings for all they are worth. Amen.

● ● ● **Act on it!**

Could you leave a small gift of food on somebody's doorstep today to let them know that they are loved? It could be a homemade cake or a jar of their favourite jam – the main thing is that it will make them smile!

Story 13

Unabashed

> At that time the disciples came to Jesus and asked, 'Who, then, is the greatest in the kingdom of heaven?' He called a little child to him and placed the child among them. And he said: 'Truly I tell you, unless you change and become like little children, you will never enter the kingdom of heaven. Therefore, whoever takes the lowly position of this child is the greatest in the kingdom of heaven.
>
> *(Matt. 18:1-4)*

Sometimes people have a military bearing, long after they have left the ranks of the army. There is something about the way they stand and walk and hold themselves. Others have a regal manner, gliding through any room or crowd, as if they expect everyone in the room to defer to them. Others seem to hug the walls and melt into the shadows, as if they would rather not be seen. With Almaz it was none of those things. With her, it was an overwhelming sense that she felt at home, untroubled by whatever was going on about her. She was not self-important, in fact quite the opposite. There was a deference about her which bordered on shyness. However, beneath it all was a quiet reassurance that she somehow mattered.

Since that milestone day where she had been picked out of the crowd, life had thrown all kinds of misfortune her way. She had been entangled by poverty and scarred by disappointment like so many others. Now, with her grey hair and her stooped shoulders she seemed a million miles from that shy, smiling child who had stood at Jesus' side. And yet, through it all she knew *who she was*.

These days, others would seek her out. Those who had lost sight of themselves and lost all hope of heaven's door would come looking for Almaz, that little girl who had stood quietly beside Jesus as he made his point. Hesitatingly, they would enquire as to whether heaven really was meant for such as them, or whether God's door would be yet another which was shut in their faces. Every single time she would reassure them that the door would indeed open to all whose hearts were his.

I used to see her, walking with a stoop now, making her way through the market or stopping in the street to listen, head on one side, to a neighbour. For many months now there has been no sight of her. I know I shall see her again, though. I just know it. Jesus said so.

● ● ● Pause to reflect

Very often, we are quick to forget the sensation when we first realise that we matter to God. Instead, we experience it once again through the eyes of others who come to faith.

Prayer

Dear God, I thank you for my welcome into the kingdom of heaven, and I take it to heart today with all the simplicity of a child. Some days it is easy to believe, and others not, but help me to hold onto it, always, I pray. Amen.

● ● ● Act on it!

If you were to write a postcard to God, thanking him for 'finding' you – what would it say? Why not have a go? You may not be able to post it, but writing it is what matters.

Story 14

Mr and Mrs Pilate

While Pilate was sitting on the judge's seat, his wife sent him this message: 'Don't have anything to do with that innocent man, for I have suffered a great deal today in a dream because of him.' But the chief priests and the elders persuaded the crowd to ask for Barabbas and to have Jesus executed. 'Which of the two do you want me to release to you?' asked the governor. 'Barabbas,' they answered. 'What shall I do, then, with Jesus who is called the Messiah?' Pilate asked. They all answered, 'Crucify him!' 'Why? What crime has he committed?' asked Pilate. But they shouted all the louder, 'Crucify him!' When Pilate saw that he was getting nowhere, but that instead an uproar was starting, he took water and washed his hands in front of the crowd. 'I am innocent of this man's blood,' he said. 'It is your responsibility!'

(Matt. 27:19-24)

Things were distinctly frosty when Pilate headed back to his temporary residence in the Praetorium that night. To be honest, they were never that good here anyway. Jerusalem was dusty and noisy, it lacked the sea breezes of Caesarea Maritima, and when all was said and done, this was more military fortress than palace. Every time they came here on official business, rolling in through the city gates with all the pomp and vulgarity of a circus, they were counting the days until they could return.

The accommodation was not the problem on this occasion, though. He did not need to tell her what had happened. On hearing the roar of the crowd, she would have needed only to look out of the window to see Barabbas and his hooligan supporters barrelling up the street whooping and shouting. After that had come a much sadder procession. At its head, Jesus of Nazareth, bruised and bleeding, scarcely able to bear his own weight, let alone that of a heavy cross. If she had watched long enough, she would have seen a visitor from Cyrene pressed into service to carry the wretched thing to the top of the hill. After that, she would have watched no longer. You could see the crosses from the fortress, but she had no appetite for Roman bloodletting.

In his heart he had rehearsed many times what he would say. There had been time to dwell on the injured pride and anger at having an unsolicited note passed to him on the judgement seat. This was a moment for a more conciliatory approach. He would explain that whilst his power was great, it was not unlimited. From that – he would have gone on to describe the temple people as they muttered and pointed, and the crowd whipped up like hounds baying for blood. It would have been uncomfortable and made him feel foolish, but it could have eased things.

They ate in angry silence. At the end of the meal, she carefully picked up the olive stones and pips they had left on the table and pushed them angrily towards him on a plate of silver as she rose to leave. There were thirty of them.

● ● ● **Pause to reflect**

It is often said that guilt is a wasted emotion, but it need not be if it leads to repentance and resolve.

Prayer

Dear God, when the heat is on, and I feel exposed to the scrutiny of others, help me to do the right thing at the right time, I pray. Amen.

● ● ● Act on it!

Review your diary for the next few days. What are the moments when you may find yourself needing to make difficult choices about what to say or how to act?

Story 15

Up and At It

As soon as they left the synagogue, they went with James and John to the home of Simon and Andrew. Simon's mother-in-law was in bed with a fever, and they immediately told Jesus about her. So he went to her, took her hand and helped her up. The fever left her and she began to wait on them.

(Mark 1:29–31)

The first thing Anna noticed, as her vision began to clear, was that the boys were here. Of course, Simon and Andrew had long since stopped being boys – but to her they would always be that. To find herself lying down on the bed in the middle of the day when they turned up was embarrassing, but at least they were not 'proper' company. To her shame, as she began to sit up, she noticed that they were not alone. At least she knew James and John, though, so perhaps they would forgive her being such a terrible host. It was only a flicker of kindly John's eyes to the left which made her realise that someone was still holding her hand. Hardly daring to raise her eyes, she saw that it was the teacher, Jesus, who was holding it. Why was he doing that, she wondered?

Straight away she covered her embarrassment by shooing the men away from the bed and insisting that they sit and wait for some food which she would surely prepare. Whatever would her neighbours think if they knew that she, Anna, had guests in her house and had been sleeping when they arrived? She was glad to hear the sound of their chatter and laughter behind her as she bustled around amongst the pots and pans to find whatever she could. Judging by the state of her supplies, it must have been days since she had visited the market, and she wondered why. It was then that it dawned on her. She had not been sleeping, but sick. Days and nights had passed in a fever which had pushed her to the edge and would not let her rise from bed. It was over now, though, and in a short time there was bread warm from the griddle, plump olives, and an earthenware flagon of rough red wine on the table.

As the honoured guest, it fell to Jesus to thank God for his provision. Out of the corner of her eye, she watched as he held the bread aloft and prayed with glad confidence to the God who had nurtured the barley and given skills to the miller who made the flour. Had those hands, spread wide in blessing, really been the ones which healed her not half an hour before?

Prayer over, he tore the flatbread, still warm, and handed pieces to the boys. She had seen men do that in this house a thousand times before – but on this occasion a shiver ran up her spine as she watched him do it, and she wondered why.

● ● ● Pause to reflect

We might feel that Simon's mother-in-law needed a rest after her experiences, rather than rushing straight off to the kitchen! However, often people *want to* act on their gratitude, rather than simply expressing it in words.

Prayer

Dear God, I pray that someone who cries out to you from the depths of their heart for healing might receive it. Please let no one feel today that they are beyond your reach, no matter how dark things may get. Amen.

● ● ● Act on it!

Whilst this is the story of a miraculous healing, many are involved in healing others through their hard work and skills. Could you drop a thank-you card into your local GP surgery or hospital today, or maybe to a nurse or carer known to you?

Story 16

The House with a Hole in the Roof

Some men came, bringing to him a paralysed man, carried by four of them. Since they could not get him to Jesus because of the crowd, they made an opening in the roof above Jesus by digging through it and then lowered the mat the man was lying on. When Jesus saw their faith, he said to the paralysed man, 'Son, your sins are forgiven.' Now some teachers of the law were sitting there, thinking to themselves, 'Why does this fellow talk like that? He's blaspheming! Who can forgive sins but God alone?' Immediately Jesus knew in his spirit that this was what they were thinking in their hearts, and he said to them, 'Why are you thinking these things? Which is easier: to say to this paralysed man, 'Your sins are forgiven,' or to say, 'Get up, take your mat and walk'? But I want you to know that the Son of Man has authority on earth to forgive sins.' So, he said to the man, 'I tell you, get up, take your mat and go home.' He got up, took his mat and walked out in full view of them all . . .

(Mark 2:3–12)

After all the excitement of the teaching and the healing, people gradually began to drift away from the house. For those few hours, this humble place had been at the epicentre of a spiritual earthquake as hearts and lives had been changed. Now it was just a small house again, with a large hole in the roof. For the first few days, we left it. The weather was fair, and it wasn't doing any harm. Our house had become different because of it, and we rather liked it. At certain times of day, the sun would fall through the hole and project a puddle of light, right there where it had happened. It was like a rug made of sunlight. To stand on the edge of it was to feel the warmth of the sun on the back of your neck and its echo from the beaten earth beneath your feet. I suppose it was a kind of 'X marks the spot', lest we should ever forget.

To be honest, we stood in it only rarely, maybe just a tentative toe or foot, as if dipping it in that shiny pool. It felt a little too sacred to simply stand there as if it were an ordinary patch of floor. After all, heaven had touched earth in that place. At a word from the man Jesus, sins had rolled away right here. Legs dormant since birth had stretched out and found their strength, as if they had just been waiting for somebody to tell them. What a place!

Of course, over time the roof got mended, sun was replaced with shade, and we would go to and fro across the spot as if nothing had ever happened. All the same, in moments of heaviness and when no one was looking, I would press the sole of my foot onto that patch of beaten earth. I would feel its echoed warmth creep into me and whisper a prayer to the God of my life. In that house, no one ever doubted that he was listening.

● ● ● Pause to reflect

This was an ordinary house turned into a sacred space because of what happened there. Are there ordinary places made extraordinary for you because of what God did there?

What Happened Next?

> **Prayer**

Dear God, as I reflect right now on wonderful answers to prayer which you have given in the past, I ask that I might pray big prayers for the future. Amen.

● ● ● **Act on it!**

If possible, go and visit a place which God has made sacred to you today. If you can't get there physically, then revisit it in your mind and thank God for what he did there.

Story 17

The Girl with an Appetite

> After he put them all out, he took the child's father and mother and the disciples who were with him and went in where the child was. He took her by the hand and said to her, '*Talitha koum!*' (which means 'Little girl, I say to you, get up!'). Immediately the girl stood up and began to walk around (she was twelve years old). At this they were completely astonished. He gave strict orders not to let anyone know about this, and told them to give her something to eat.
>
> *(Mark 5:40-43)*

My name's not Talitha, of course. Talitha is a pet name, the kind of name you call a little girl when she's still getting her tongue around her real name and can't quite manage it. For me, though, that name has lingered all the way through the years. It is almost as if I had a second 'naming ceremony' there in that darkened room in that house full of sadness. After that, my parents went on using it to keep the memory of that sacred day alive, and now even my grandchildren use it, racing around my knee and grinning up at me as they do it. Grandma the 'poppet'!

Along with the name – something else has always stayed with me: I'm always hungry. No matter how recently I've eaten – there always seems to be a little space to fill. When people tease me about it, I tell them every time – Jesus said, 'give her something to eat' and I have been cashing in on it ever since. After all, to have divine approval for such a thing is not to be lightly dismissed! Joking apart, though – I may feel more peckish than most, but my soul is full, and my heart satisfied every single day.

He *touched* me. He reached down into the clammy pool of death and plucked me out again – and now every day is an unexpected gift. When I look back at my years now, at the husband I loved and the children I bore, I am so grateful. But for Jesus, my life would have been over before it had barely begun. My parents would have buried their little 'poppet' and grieved for the rest of their days.

Of course, my days will run out some time, I know that. One day this 'poppet' will fall asleep and wake somewhere quite different. I like to think that when I do, I shall wake up and see him leaning over my bed as he did once before, telling me to 'get up'. When he does, I shall have a spring in my step, the like of which I have never known.

● ● ● Pause to reflect

In many cultures, people receive a new name when they are baptised as believers – such as 'Grace', 'Mercy' or 'Hope'. I have often wondered what mine might have been. What about you?

The Girl with an Appetite

Prayer

Dear God, so quickly days pass into weeks and weeks into months without us 'measuring' them as we should. Help me to savour the blessings of every single day as precious gifts from you, I pray. Amen.

Act on it!

Think of someone known to you whose life was changed forever by an encounter with Jesus. Why not get in touch to remind them of how powerful their story is? Maybe you could encourage them to tell it to someone today?

Story 18

The Homecoming

> As Jesus was getting into the boat, the man who had been demon-possessed begged to go with him. Jesus did not let him, but said, 'Go home to your own people and tell them how much the Lord has done for you, and how he has had mercy on you.' So the man went away and began to tell in the Decapolis how much Jesus had done for him. And all the people were amazed.
>
> *(Mark 5:18–20)*

Without really realising she had done it; she had kept his space. It was not a room: nobody had a room in this tiny house. All the same, it was his corner. Look – there was the thinning pile of straw on which he had slept, a dent still in the middle as if only just vacated. There was his cloak, the one with a hole in it where he had plunged his hand into the fire at the bidding of a voice which no one but him had ever heard. There was his little stick, gnarled head carved into a mocking face, not unlike his own. Every week she would tend these objects as if curating a museum to his memory. She would shake the dust from the cloak, push the edges of the straw back into place, and polish the face on the gnarled stick, shuddering a little at what had become of his.

Of course, he wasn't *that* far away – down there among the tombstones at the water's edge, but it could have been another country altogether. When friends and neighbours had

The Homecoming

dragged him away to chain him there, she had not argued. The demons in his head had damaged the family outside it and he had to go. All their lives were in danger if he stayed, and she knew it was so. All the same, there was a tenderness to this little act of repeated devotion, a homage to the man who once had been.

Today, she had just finished for this week, when there was a commotion outside. She could hear the scuffling of feet, the odd pail and broom knocked over in haste as people rushed to the edge of the dusty road. 'He's coming, he's coming!' they cried, and looked anxiously in her direction. By now, the children were gathered at her skirts, peering around her at all the excitement and commotion. She wondered whoever they were talking about. Was it some famous rabbi, or even the man Jesus that everybody was talking about, she wondered?

And then, the crowd parted, and he stood there. In his face was a kindness she had long since forgotten. Around the corners of his eyes was a smile which once had melted her heart. He looked upright, and free and . . . beautiful. When the children rushed towards their half-remembered daddy, she did not try to stop them. He. Was. Home.

● ● ● Pause to reflect

I have often found this story hard to read, because it seems harsh to turn the man away when he wants so very much to stay with Jesus. For every believer, there will be times when God's guidance seems harsh, or puzzling or both.

Prayer

Dear God, for anybody who anticipates reconciliation with equal measures of dread and hope, I pray today. Amen.

● ● ● Act on it!

One of the least discussed challenges of military service is that of coming home. Many who have served in the Armed Forces find the adjustment to home life to be exceptionally challenging. Pray for the chaplains and others who help with this adjustment. Resolve today to find out more about a charity which helps with this, and maybe think about supporting them. For example, see Walking With The Wounded – https://walkingwiththewounded.org.uk/

Story 19

The Abandoned Cloak

Then they came to Jericho. As Jesus and his disciples, together with a large crowd, were leaving the city, a blind man, Bartimaeus (which means 'son of Timaeus'), was sitting by the roadside begging. When he heard that it was Jesus of Nazareth, he began to shout, 'Jesus, Son of David, have mercy on me!' Many rebuked him and told him to be quiet, but he shouted all the more, 'Son of David, have mercy on me!' Jesus stopped and said, 'Call him.' So, they called to the blind man, 'Cheer up! On your feet! He's calling you.' Throwing his cloak aside, he jumped to his feet and came to Jesus. 'What do you want me to do for you?' Jesus asked him. The blind man said, 'Rabbi, I want to see.' 'Go,' said Jesus, 'your faith has healed you.' Immediately he received his sight and followed Jesus along the road.

(Mark 10:46–52)

Do I remember Bartimaeus? Of course I remember Bartimaeus. Everybody remembers Bartimaeus. Many of us grew up with him as a fixture on this particular corner of the road. Every day, even high days and holy days, he would be here begging for alms. I suppose he could feel his way here along the buildings and past the gnarled olive tree on the corner. They do that, don't they? The blind use their fingers as eyes and feel their way across the earth. Each day he would reach his spot, unlace his cloak, set it on the ground, and sit down on it – a bit like setting up his stall for the day. I don't suppose he ever knew what colour it was, did he?

What Happened Next?

I did, though. Often, I had admired its hue and the fine weave of its threads. What a shame, I thought, that its wearer never gets to see its qualities. At least he never got to see the dust all across it at the end of each day, though. Would he even know it if he saw it about my shoulders now? I was there on the day when Bartimaeus found his voice and shouted down the crowd to attract the attention of Jesus as he passed by. I was there when the world stopped, and Jesus summoned him. Mine were the hands helping him to his feet and pointing him in the direction of the Saviour. Theirs was the briefest of conversations, but it changed Bartimaeus forever. From that moment he looked forward and up and around, but never back. He followed Jesus down the road to Jerusalem and left the cloak behind.

Like everybody else, I stayed around to gasp and wonder and chatter at the miracle which we had witnessed. After that – some followed Jesus and his crowd down the road, and others drifted back to their homes. I was left, quite literally, holding his cloak. I took it home, washed it, mended a tear in the hem, and now I wear it almost every day. It is not mine, of course, but I shall hold onto it until the rightful owner returns. I stand on this corner every morning hoping to catch sight of him. Of course, if I do, I shall have to cry out, since he knows my voice but has never seen my face. When he does, I shall unlace this cloak from my shoulders, drape it about his like a royal robe on the shoulders of a homecoming king and maybe ask him if he or his friend Jesus can help *me* to see things a little more clearly.

The Abandoned Cloak

● ● ● **Pause to reflect**

Sometimes our response to Jesus is so cautious, polite and measured. For Bartimaeus to leave his one valuable item of clothing behind was a measure of how profound was the impact of Jesus upon him.

Prayer

Dear God, I love to see the prayers of other people answered, like watching that blind man go off down the road sighted. Sometimes I still long for mine which are awaiting an answer, though. Maybe today could be the day? Amen.

● ● ● **Act on it!**

Find a Christian charity today who are working with those who are blind, as Bartimaeus once was, or partially sighted. For example, see the Torch Trust – https://torchtrust.org/. Pray for them, and maybe write to encourage them in their work.

Story 20

An Empty Upper Room

> While they were eating, Jesus took bread, and when he had given thanks, he broke it and gave it to his disciples, saying, 'Take it; this is my body.' Then he took a cup, and when he had given thanks, he gave it to them, and they all drank from it. 'This is my blood of the covenant, which is poured out for many,' he said to them. 'Truly I tell you; I will not drink again from the fruit of the vine until that day when I drink it new in the kingdom of God.' When they had sung a hymn, they went out to the Mount of Olives.
>
> *(Mark 14:22-26)*

It was always awkward to know when to clear the room upstairs if there were guests in. Sometimes things would go quiet, and he would pad softly upstairs to begin clearing away, only to discover that they were silently praying. On another occasion, he had assumed that they were finished and gone in to start clearing, but then found that they had simply gone outside for a breather, and they startled him when they came back in. He would have been horrified to think that anyone thought he was the kind of host who would want his guests to leave before they were ready.

On this occasion, he sensed that there was something special about these guests and hung back. To his shame, he had deliberately poked his head out of the downstairs window to try to catch some of their conversation. It had only come in snatches, though, and made little sense. Long into the evening, when the last embers of the sun had been replaced by silver moonlight, he heard the sound of them singing a hymn together. It was a familiar Passover hymn but sounded unbelievably sad on this occasion. As the last notes faded away, he heard their feet coming down the stairs one after the other, and then all fell silent.

After a decent interval, he made his way up the stairs to collect the cups and clear up after the meal. He was not a sentimental man, but the room felt almost radiant, as if heaven had kissed earth, right here in his house. Shaking his head to clear such foolish thoughts, he went to the head of the table and saw a rounded flatbread torn neatly in half, the two pieces lying next to each other just so, like a broken heart. Running down the outside of the simple clay goblet at that place was a drop of wine, looking for all the world like a trickle of blood. In the most ordinary gesture, he slid his finger up the ridges of clay to wipe it off and saw that his finger was stained by the rich red wine. It still is today.

● ● ● Pause to reflect

The man at the heart of this story has an anonymous 'bit part' in the great narrative of salvation, and yet the things which went on in his room are remembered in every church of every denomination to this day.

What Happened Next?

Prayer

Dear God, I thank you for the words of Jesus around that table and for the new covenant in his blood which changed everything. Although I couldn't be there to see it for myself, I thank you that I can touch and taste it for myself in bread and wine. Amen.

● ● ● Act on it!

Who is responsible in your church for making preparations for bread and wine to be shared in worship? How can you thank them today?

Story 21

The Centurion Who Saw

With a loud cry, Jesus breathed his last. The curtain of the temple was torn in two from top to bottom. And when the centurion, who stood there in front of Jesus, saw how he died, he said, 'Surely this man was the Son of God!'

(Mark 15:37-39)

When military service is done and the emperor allows a man to return to his home, he does so with pride. Shoulder to shoulder he has fought alongside others to expand the empire and carry Caesar's name to the wide world. Most keep a souvenir of that glorious time, and I have seen so many homes with a battered helmet in the hearth, or a scarred sword propped in the corner.

In mine, where those things should be, there is a small earthenware bowl, and in it a pile of Judean earth, dry and dusty now after all these years. My servant knows he dare not throw it out and must clean round it as reverently as if it were a gift from the gods. I scooped that earth from the ground between my two feet as I stood in the pitch dark in the middle of the day on a hillside outside Jerusalem many, many years ago.

I had seen so many crucifixions. It was a gruesome job, and one they gave to the men who were older now, and no longer suited to frontline fighting. Often it could take many hours, and I would glance up from time to time into the faces of the victims to see how things were going. When I looked up at this one, though, I saw something I had never seen before – strength. It was not bravado, the last flash of life. Not at all. This man was defiant, as if he were reaching some kind of beginning rather than an end. With breath that came from somewhere deep inside, he shouted at the top of his voice that it was finished, then bowed his head and was gone. With that the earth shook, the sky went black, and I dropped down to grab that fistful of earth. As I straightened up, the soldier beside me told me that I said with all the confidence in the world, 'Truly this man was the Son of God!' It was not the kind of thing a centurion is meant to say, and I swore him to keep quiet about it until I was safely home.

Many things have changed now, and that man on the cross is the Lord of my life, holding more sway over me than the emperor ever did. Whenever the church gathers here in my little house, they know not to overturn that little dish and its precious contents.

● ● ● Pause to reflect

When I first came to faith, I was very envious of those whose response to God was a dramatic one, like the one in this story. In truth, it does not matter how we come, as long as we do.

Prayer

Dear God, today I thank you for those little moments of revelation when you have revealed a special something to me about yourself. Help me to understand their value, and to see them for the precious treasures which they are. Amen.

● ● ● Act on it!

We should never worship objects, but are there objects in your house which remind you of something special which God has done, like the bowl of earth in the story? If so, hold one in your hand as you thank God.

Story 22

A Lifetime of Shame

> So Joseph also went up from the town of Nazareth in Galilee to Judea, to Bethlehem the town of David, because he belonged to the house and line of David. He went there to register with Mary, who was pledged to be married to him and was expecting a child. While they were there, the time came for the baby to be born, and she gave birth to her firstborn, a son. She wrapped him in cloths and placed him in a manger, because there was no guest room available for them.
>
> *(Luke 2:4–7)*

Jerusalem was a city awash with holy sites. There were stones dressed by Nehemiah, others selected by Solomon, and the great temple itself. For a canny salesman, there was always money to be made from a brush with the holy. Even the smallest connection was enough to guarantee an income.

In Bethlehem, it was not the same thing at all. It was a small place with very few claims to fame that could rival its majestic neighbour. Anyone who found such a thing would exploit it for all it was worth. In fact, not everyone, it would seem. Abel and his family had run a tavern in this part of town for generations. It was an unassuming place but known for its simple food and warm welcome. Many of the guests were regulars, who would come back year after year whenever their travels brought them this way. There were three rooms for overnight stays, together with one for Abel and his wife.

A Lifetime of Shame

Out the back was a lean-to store where the amphorae were stacked, and beyond that an animal house with a manger and some tired-looking straw. *That* was where the problem lay.

Of course, for many years it was dangerous to talk of the little life which started there and the visitors who came and went. When the madness had died down, though, it would have been fine. Any one of Abel's neighbours would have roped off the animal house, charged people to look at it, and then had a stonemason enclose it with the money that came rolling in. Over time, Abel could have stopped serving meals and pouring drinks. His grown-up children could have taken the other three rooms and looked after him into his old age. He would not do it, though. He seemed to want to make others comfortable, even at cost to himself, and would do so until God took his last breath.

Sometimes when the food was good and comforting and the red wine had flowed, people would get him to talk about that night. All at once, the face of the smiling host would darken. His booming voice would drop to a hoarse whisper, and he would hang his head as an old and unwelcome visitor stalked from memory to lips. Its name was shame. Try as he might, he could not erase the shame that he had slept that fateful night in his warm bed whilst the Messiah of God had nestled under the rarely changed straw outside. Would anyone ever remember him without dismay? Would there be room for a little compassion, he wondered, whenever his tale was told?

What Happened Next?

◉ ◉ ◉ **Pause to reflect**

The innkeeper has become a two-dimensional part in any Nativity play – either opening the door or not, depending on which innkeeper they are playing. Wouldn't it gnaw at you, though, to know that you could have had the Messiah of God under your roof and put them in the stable instead?

Prayer

Dear God, everyone reading this page has made mistakes, and done things which we would rather undo. I pray that we might find forgiveness from you and for ourselves today. Amen.

◉ ◉ ◉ **Act on it!**

It is always good to plan to do something good for a neighbour. Today, why not stop planning and actually do it? It could be anything from sharing a cup of tea with them to running an errand for them.

Story 23

All the Way Home

> So they hurried off and found Mary and Joseph, and the baby, who was lying in the manger. When they had seen him, they spread the word concerning what had been told them about this child, and all who heard it were amazed at what the shepherds said to them. But Mary treasured up all these things and pondered them in her heart. The shepherds returned, glorifying and praising God for all the things they had heard and seen, which were just as they had been told.
>
> *(Luke 2:16–20)*

You can generally tell where shepherds have walked through a town or village, as they leave a certain 'aroma' behind them. It is a heady combination of grubby sheep, unwashed clothes and equally unwashed bodies. A quick splash in a brook running down a hillside is no substitute for a proper wash, and there is a reason that shepherds tend to live a life apart in every way. On this occasion, though, they seemed to leave a trail of another kind altogether. In each village and hamlet and farmstead through which they passed on the way back to the hills they somehow left the indelible mark of joy behind them.

In some places there were neighbours who usually ignored each other, talking with great animation to one another. In others, there were individuals who looked for all the world as if every promise they had ever held dear had all been kept at once. One or two even had that combination of deathly pale and rosy glow which sits on the face of a person who has met an angel. Something wonderful had happened in those places that night, and the shepherds had left a trail of surprise and joy behind them, which was something of a novelty.

As dawn started to dilute the night sky at the edges with the first hint of pink, the shepherds left the villages behind them and made their way to the more familiar territory of the hills. To see their arms waving as they went, you would have thought they were dancing all the way. A curious boy from one of the villages decided to follow them from a distance, and the story of what he saw has been passed down through the generations ever since.

When they got back to the flocks, none of whom had wandered, they sat down before them as if addressing an audience in a theatre. Tripping over each other in their enthusiasm to get the tale out, they recounted the night's adventures. The boy said those sheep sat and listened as if they understood every word. Can it really be? Stranger things have happened . . .

● ● ● **Pause to reflect**

Shepherds were held personally responsible for the safety of the sheep under their care. To leave them unattended and head off to Bethlehem, even at the bidding of an angel, was a brave thing to do.

Prayer

Dear God, I thank you for the irrepressible joy of those shepherds. By obeying the angel and heading to Bethlehem they saw such wonderful things. Today, I pray that I might carry such joy with me wherever I go. Amen.

● ● ● Act on it!

Whose story of faith has moved you recently? Have you told them so? Why not do that today?

Story 24

Mother's Boy

Soon afterwards, Jesus went to a town called Nain, and his disciples and a large crowd went along with him. As he approached the town gate, a dead person was being carried out – the only son of his mother, and she was a widow. And a large crowd from the town was with her. When the Lord saw her, his heart went out to her and he said, 'Don't cry.' Then he went up and touched the bier they were carrying him on, and the bearers stood still. He said, 'Young man, I say to you, get up!' The dead man sat up and began to talk, and Jesus gave him back to his mother.
(Luke 7:11–15)

Holding onto his mother's shoulder for a moment to steady himself, the young man started to look around and wondered why he was here. He could see there was a crowd, and sense that something had happened, but he had no idea what. Odder still, there was a bier in the middle of the crowd with no body on it. The shroud lay in a crumpled heap on the floor, as if discarded. More out of habit than anything, he picked it up as it seemed disrespectful to the dead to leave it there. Unsure what to do with this awkward garment, he handed it to his mother as he had done with so many things since the sickness had set in. She smiled at him as he did so, as if he were handing her a beautiful garment rather than a shroud for the dead. Oddly, too, he no longer felt sick.

As the crowd began to melt away, she took him by the elbow and began to steer him home. He found the stares of friends and neighbours most unnerving as they passed by, but she seemed to lap them up, like an athlete collecting plaudits from the crowd. He truly could not remember when he had last seen her this happy. Come to think of it, there were many things he could not remember. He could not remember why he was not at work that day, manhandling blocks of stone and chipping away at them as his father had done before him. He could not remember why he and his mother were out in the town in the middle of the day without apparently being on the way to market. He also could not remember when he last ate and began to quicken his pace at the prospect of eating his mother's food.

It turns out that her mind was on food too. She had friends who had friends who were sure to know Jesus, the man who had touched her son and woken him from the last sleep. She would not rest now until she had invited him to her home, fed him her food, and said at least a thousand thank yous.

● ● ● Pause to reflect

When a person's life is touched dramatically by God, we celebrate it as a good thing, which it is. However, we should remember that adjusting to the new reality may be a considerable challenge.

What Happened Next?

Prayer

Dear God, so often my thanks are brief, over in a heartbeat and soon forgotten. Today, I pray that things may be different and that my thanks would linger in my heart and mind all day. Amen.

● ● ● Act on it!

Is there some way today that you could *demonstrate* your thanks to God, rather than just saying it?

Story 25

After the Perfume

> Then he turned toward the woman and said to Simon, 'Do you see this woman? I came into your house. You did not give me any water for my feet, but she wet my feet with her tears and wiped them with her hair. You did not give me a kiss, but this woman, from the time I entered, has not stopped kissing my feet. You did not put oil on my head, but she has poured perfume on my feet. Therefore, I tell you, her many sins have been forgiven – as her great love has shown. But whoever has been forgiven little loves little.' Then Jesus said to her, 'Your sins are forgiven.'
>
> The other guests began to say among themselves, 'Who is this who even forgives sins?' Jesus said to the woman, 'Your faith has saved you; go in peace.'
>
> **(Luke 7:44-50)**

. . . and with that, she rose to her feet, picked up the vial of perfume and its little stopper, and made her way out of the house. Without looking back at Jesus or the other dinner guests, she made her way from the house. On her way she left a trail of scent behind her every bit as obvious as a line of muddy footprints would have been. It seemed to follow her, leaving in its wake a heady mix of disgust, astonishment, amusement and shock.

Walking into the house, her head had been covered and bowed and she had hugged the wall, as if seeking to enter unseen. Now, it was a different story. Head held high and hair loosed, she smiled the kind of smile which the muscles in her face had forgotten, and walked away from the house. For the first time in as long as she could remember, she felt unashamed – a true daughter of Abraham once again. She clutched the vial tightly in her hand and vowed that it would never leave her side for all her days. Somehow it felt more precious empty than it ever had full. If she never owned another valuable thing all her life, this would be enough.

Meanwhile, in the Pharisee's house, the party was starting to break up. People made excuses, remembered vital appointments elsewhere, and beat a hasty retreat from that house reeking of sweet perfume and bitter shame. One or two looked at each other and raised a cynical eyebrow, others found that they could only look at the floor, and nobody would look the host in the eye.

He would not have seen anyway.

Simon's eyes were fixed on Jesus, and he felt as if he might shed a tear at any minute. Did he really understand the heart of God so little, after all these years? Had he really been told that he loved so little, he wondered? Was that the point of this outlandish display and the stinging story which followed it? In general, a host seeks compliments when the meal draws to a close, but all he wanted was absolution.

● ● ● Pause to reflect

There is a word in German, *schadenfreude*, which means 'delight in the shame of others'. If I had been a guest at Simon's table, I wonder whether I would have felt it on that occasion?

Prayer

Dear God, sometimes I wonder whether I realise how much I have truly been forgiven by you? Give me a little bit of insight today, that I might be grateful from the top of my head to the tips of my toes, I pray. Amen.

● ● ● Act on it!

Find a way to give to someone or something today, where there is no prospect of thanks or reward. That way, it is an act of pure gratitude to God on your part.

Story 26

The Tale of an Inn (1)

> A man was going down from Jerusalem to Jericho, when he was attacked by robbers. They stripped him of his clothes, beat him and went away, leaving him half-dead. A priest happened to be going down the same road, and when he saw the man, he passed by on the other side. So too, a Levite, when he came to the place and saw him, passed by on the other side. But a Samaritan, as he travelled, came where the man was; and when he saw him, he took pity on him. He went to him and bandaged his wounds, pouring on oil and wine. Then he put the man on his own donkey, brought him to an inn and took care of him. The next day he took out two denarii and gave them to the innkeeper. 'Look after him,' he said, 'and when I return, I will reimburse you for any extra expense you may have.'
>
> *(Luke 10:30-35)*

I had never intended to go into the hospitality business. Inns were places where I stayed, and nothing more. I would pass through on business on my way from town to town looking for a meal, or sometimes a bed, but that was it. Sometimes I would look at the innkeeper scurrying from kitchen to table or sweeping the dust from the road out through the door again and again, and wonder at such unforgiving work. The fact that I am doing it now, in the very inn where I stayed on that fateful journey, is a tale all of its own.

After I had recovered, I went on my way, but would change my business trips just so that I could come here. Time and

The Tale of an Inn (1)

time again I would be drawn to this place, like a moth to a lamp or a thirsty man to a cool spring. I had been mended and healed here, you see, and I could not keep away. I had been carried in here battered and bleeding, my body barely clinging to life. It took many weeks and much costly care to set me back on my feet again.

As the years went by, the innkeeper became a friend, and when he got too old to care for the place any more, I offered to buy it from him. He gladly agreed, said that it felt like passing it on to an old friend, and moved away to live with his children.

So here I am now, scurrying from kitchen to table and sweeping the dust from the road every time it comes unbidden through the door. Those little tasks never irk me as I thought they would. No matter how many times I do them, each time it feels like a gift of sorts to my guests. A long time ago a stranger on that road out there taught me the value of generosity, and I intend to live the rest of my days by it.

● ● ● Pause to reflect

I sometimes wish the Samaritan in this story had a name. Then again, maybe he has thousands of names – the name of every person who has ever imitated his good deeds.

Prayer

Dear God, I thank you for those whose generosity has blessed me in the past. Nudged by you, they have helped me in a hundred and one different ways. Give them a blessing today, I pray. Amen.

Act on it!

The road to recovery for this man would probably have been a long one, after such trauma. Remember those who are long-term carers, living a life of self-sacrifice for the sake of another person. Is there anyone you know who cares for others, that you could bless today?

Story 27

The Tale of an Inn (2)

> As he was going into a village, ten men who had leprosy met him. They stood at a distance and called out in a loud voice, 'Jesus, Master, have pity on us!' When he saw them, he said, 'Go, show yourselves to the priests.' And as they went, they were cleansed. One of them, when he saw he was healed, came back, praising God in a loud voice. He threw himself at Jesus' feet and thanked him – and he was a Samaritan.
> *(Luke 17:12–16)*

On the outskirts of the village, just when you think there is no further hope of food or drink, there is a small tavern. Outside, a sign swings in the very occasional breeze bearing the name, *One of Ten*. The name is not the only unusual thing about this place. There is no pricelist, either. Those who stop here for food and drink are invited to pay whatever they can, even if that is nothing. The owner beams as if he has received the greatest gift even when some poor soul slides only a mite across the counter to pay for his meal. And to add to it all, this beaming host, full of bonhomie, is a Samaritan far from home.

On the day he had come to this town, he had only been passing through – as his kind tend to do. In fact, it would be fairer to say he was passing *by* – since lepers of any hue are not welcome in the town itself. He and some others had gathered on this corner, hoping for alms but not expecting it. When they shouted and bellowed at Jesus to pay them

What Happened Next?

heed, none of them had the slightest notion that he might actually do so. After he had spoken to them, they set off in the direction of the priests, though they only did it so as not to seem ungrateful to the teacher. Nobody actually thought anything had changed. Of course, as they went – it was a different story. One, then another and another looked down and realised that the angry red welts and the flaking skin which had been their curse for as long as they could remember were gone. In their place was the clear skin of the healthy.

Most scattered at that point, running off to tell kin and long-forgotten families that all was well. Only the Samaritan returned, kneeling at Jesus' feet and gazing up at him in thanks. When Jesus and his followers finally moved on, he stood, watching them until the distance swallowed them up. After that, he stayed, and then stayed some more – as if he could not quite bear to leave the spot where his life had changed. He ended up buying this little scrap of land on the street corner and building the place himself, brick by brick. If you ask him about the pricelist thing he will just smile and shrug, saying that any free drink or meal he gives away is just the smallest dent in an unpayable debt.

● ● ● **Pause to reflect**

We shall never know why the other nine men in this story did not come back to offer their thanks. It may have been excitement, as they were so caught up in the joy of their healing that they forgot. It may have been embarrassment, since they could never thank Jesus enough for doing such a thing. Whatever motives we might imagine, it is probably true to say that each of them has applied to us on some occasion when God has answered a prayer.

Prayer

Dear God, as someone who has been blessed by you out of all proportion, I pray that you would inspire me to acts of beautiful generosity today. If there is someone whom I have forgotten to thank, then I pray that you would bring them to mind right now. Amen.

● ● ● Act on it!

Since this story features ten lepers, take a piece of paper and write the numbers 1 to 10 down one side. Now write one thing next to each number for which you are thankful today. They might vary from the physical to the spiritual, but all are blessings from God.

Story 28

Tree House

> A man was there by the name of Zacchaeus; he was a chief tax collector and was wealthy. He wanted to see who Jesus was, but because he was short, he could not see over the crowd. So he ran ahead and climbed a sycamore-fig tree to see him, since Jesus was coming that way. When Jesus reached the spot, he looked up and said to him, 'Zacchaeus, come down immediately. I must stay at your house today.' So he came down at once and welcomed him gladly.
>
> *(Luke 19:2-6)*

It is many years now since Zacchaeus moved to this house. It is still on the main road to Jericho, but further out, where the cheaper houses are to be found. After that day with Jesus, he gave so much away that the big house felt empty and pointless. Of course, he could have gone right back and earned it all over again, but he had no appetite for it. Instead, he stopped working for the Province, sold his house, and left it behind with a glad heart and a slightly emptier pocket.

His neighbours in the poorer neighbourhood were surprised when he moved in. After all, they all knew him. *Everybody* knew him (and most people avoided him). At first, they avoided him too, as nobody could really believe he had changed so much. As the years came and went, though, all could see that the change went all the way from the top of his head to the roots of his soul. Eventually they would come to treat him as one of their own, which he had never been before.

The one thing they couldn't get their heads around was the sapling he brought with him when he moved. Sycamores can be such a nuisance with their falling leaves and their indestructible roots, so why would anybody want to plant one? Not only did he plant it, but he cared for it as if it were his very own child. He trimmed it and watered it and fed it and there were rumours that he even spoke to it, quietly, when no one was looking.

By the time it had grown to the height of his house, Zaccheus was too old to do much more, and definitely too old to mount its branches. Instead, he used some of his meagre savings to pay a carpenter to build a little house up there. Once finished, every child from all the streets around about knew that they were welcome to clamber up there and enjoy the view. He loved nothing more than to sit at the foot of the tree, watch them come and go – and tell them of the day he climbed such a tree and changed his view forever.

● ● ● Pause to reflect

In Luke's account of the encounter between Jesus and the tax collector, Zacchaeus' response in repentance is considerably more than the law required it to be. Is our response to Christ muted, reasonable or extravagant?

What Happened Next?

Prayer

Dear God, as I look back just now, I thank you for every moment in my life where I have 'bumped into' you and it has changed my view forever. Amen.

● ● ● Act on it!

Take a good look at your own life today, and ask whether you have been as repentant and generous as Zacchaeus was. Find a way that you can demonstrate your gratitude to God, either by giving or doing.

Story 29

A Sweeper's Tale

As he went along, people spread their cloaks on the road. When he came near the place where the road goes down the Mount of Olives, the whole crowd of disciples began joyfully to praise God in loud voices for all the miracles they had seen: 'Blessed is the king who comes in the name of the Lord!' 'Peace in heaven and glory in the highest!'

(Luke 19:36–38)

I have swept these streets for twenty years, and my father swept them for twenty years before that. There's little money in it, but you get to know the people as they come to and fro, and occasionally you get to keep the odd dropped coin or two. Some days it's a thankless task, when people treat you like the dirt you are trying to sweep away, but for the most part they are decent enough. At Passover time I leave it for a couple of days. With an extra few thousand people on the streets, there just wouldn't be room for the likes of me. Instead, I wait until the crowds have gone. When I see the last of the visitors traipsing out of the city gates, the city itself breathes a sigh of relief and I head out there.

Usually, the clean-up after Passover is a good one for the little extras – so many visitors and such tightly packed crowds mean that dropped coins are almost inevitable. One year, I found a whole little bag – a leather purse with enough in it to buy a little extra for the meals that week. As I turned the corner onto the main street leading up to the temple, though, I could not believe my eyes. The whole thing was covered in palm branches as far as the eye could see. Of course, there's a lot of them about in the city at this time of year – but I had never seen them strewn like this before. It was as if someone had laid them down like a carpet.

As if that weren't strange enough, there were clothes in there too. For the most part they were cloaks – precious things. Most of the people I know only own one outer garment for travelling and colder days. Why would they throw them away like this? It was as if they had thrown them down in some kind of euphoric moment and got so carried away that they never thought to come back for them. Absent-mindedly, I started to fold each one carefully as if it were my own, and stack them at the side of the road. As the morning wore on, so the pile grew and grew.

I wasn't quite sure what to do with them, and was just wondering when a rich man, from Arimathea, came by and offered to buy every last one. He told me he was going to have them unpicked, bleached and used as grave-wrappings, which seemed like an odd thing to me. I wonder if he ever did?

● ● ● Pause to reflect

A cloak would have been a costly garment, probably the most valuable item of clothing belonging to anybody in the crowd.

A Sweeper's Tale

I often wonder what I would have laid down before Jesus if I had been there.

Prayer

Dear God, when I think of the story of that first Palm Sunday, and the crowd getting caught up in their jubilant praise, I recognise that my praise is often a tame and insipid thing. Help me to change that, I pray. Amen.

● ● ● Act on it!

The best way we can welcome King Jesus now is to welcome his servants. Next time a visitor comes to your home, what could you do to let them know how glad you are that they have come?

Story 30

After the Sacking

> When Jesus entered the temple courts, he began to drive out those who were selling. 'It is written,' he said to them, '"My house will be a house of prayer"; but you have made it "a den of robbers."' Every day he was teaching at the temple. But the chief priests, the teachers of the law and the leaders among the people were trying to kill him. Yet they could not find any way to do it, because all the people hung on his words.
>
> *(Luke 19:45–48)*

Cleaning up the temple courtyards has never been a glamorous job. You take a lot of frightened animals and a lot of jostling people and a few frayed tempers and you have a recipe for mess. Of course, nobody ever notices us. The merchants don't notice us because they have eyes only for their competitors. The public don't notice us because we arrive after they leave each day at sundown. The priests don't notice us because they have eyes only for God, or so they would have us believe. We arrive like the first shadows of evening and disappear before the first rays of the sun.

On this particular occasion, we arrived as usual to gather ourselves as trading ended for the day. The thing is, there was nobody there. Nobody. The whole place was deserted with not a merchant nor a worshipper nor even a priest in sight. Not only that, but they had abandoned it as if they left in a spectacular hurry. A cousin of mine described the scene in his village market after an earthquake, and it looked just the same. There were tables on their sides and goods tipped on the floor. Most of the animal cages were open and empty. There was one where it had trapped a dove's foot as it fell, and the poor thing was tugging at it hopelessly. When no one was looking, I let it out and my spirit soared as I watched it flap away into the blue, blue sky above the city.

Of course, the most interesting debris was around the money-changer's stalls. The coins had rolled away into every corner and trundled down the spaces between the flagstones. Many of us went home with more than a smile on our faces that day. I will be honest, and admit that I took some and spent them too. Finders, keepers. All the same, when I heard the story of what had happened that day, I kept one forever, rather than spending it. I heard all about the man who said he was Messiah sweeping into the temple like the fury of God himself and driving out the unholy trade that was there.

Each day I like to heft it in my hand before I go to do my work, and remember that temples can be beautiful places, but dangerous too if we treat them the wrong way.

● ● ● Pause to reflect

Every time I read this story, I shake my head at the shallow consumerism that had overtaken the temple. Then again, I wonder how many times I have turned the house of God into

What Happened Next?

a house of daydreaming . . . or a house of resentment when I have allowed my mind to wander?

Prayer

Dear God, please will you forgive me for those moments when I have treated holy things as less than holy? Amen.

● ● ● Act on it!

Even if it is a very familiar place, next time you are on the threshold of your church, pray before you go in that you might treat it as a holy place.

# Story 31

A Scar to Savour

> When Jesus' followers saw what was going to happen, they said, 'Lord, should we strike with our swords?' And one of them struck the servant of the high priest, cutting off his right ear. But Jesus answered, 'No more of this!' And he touched the man's ear and healed him.
>
> *(Luke 22:49–51)*

Some people like to hide their scars, as if they somehow betray a secret they would rather not share. Others sport them like badges of honour – evidence that they have plunged into the fray and emerged to tell the tale. With Malchus, it is somewhere in-between. If you get up close, you can see a neat white line between ear and neck where once his ear left his head for a moment or two. He never minds you staring, and if he sees you doing so, he is more than happy to tell the tale of how it happened.

Of course, he soon lost his job in the temple. People who had been close to Jesus in any shape or form were not welcome in such circles. Deformity was frowned upon in temple staff, even when fixed with barely a scar to show for it. And of course, if the scar was associated with some dubious healing story, it was even worse. Even if he had not been told to leave, he would probably have done it. After the things he had seen in the garden that night, he could take no pride in serving the man who was behind it all.

What Happened Next?

Malchus made new friends before long, and the followers of the man who healed him soon embraced him as part of the family. They never seemed to tire of hearing the story of that night, eyes wide as they heard again the tale of a traitor's kiss, a bright sword and a saviour's healing hand. As much as they never tired of hearing it, so Malchus never tired of telling it. That day was the start of his life, he used to say. Also, he would say, his hearing was better than it had ever been after that night – especially where the voice of God was concerned.

Of all the people in that group, the one who seemed more pleased than any to greet Malchus whenever he was in town was Peter. He would spot him from the other side of the room, hail him with a fisherman's booming voice, and make a beeline for him. Malchus was always just as pleased to see him, although funnily enough always seemed to flinch when Peter's strong arm flew around his shoulder to grab him. I wonder why?

● ● ● **Pause to reflect**

This is one of those moments in the gospel story where beauty and ugliness, violence and healing sit alongside each other. Each highlights the other.

A Scar to Savour

Prayer

Dear God, today I pray for those whose loyalty to Jesus will demand a high price of them. I know that some will stand up for Jesus at the cost of their liberty, or even their life. Stand with them, I pray. Amen.

● ● ● **Act on it!**

Every scar tells a story – I still have one on my knee from when I fell off my bike as a small boy. Any scars which you bear tell the story of a life known to God. You may have scars both inside and out. Is there one whose story you could share with someone today?

Story 32

After the Rip

> It was now about noon, and darkness came over the whole land until three in the afternoon, for the sun stopped shining. And the curtain of the temple was torn in two. Jesus called out with a loud voice, 'Father, into your hands I commit my spirit.' When he had said this, he breathed his last.
>
> *(Luke 23:44-46)*

It was very unusual for them to call us in on a festival weekend such as this. Of course, it is always a privilege to work on maintaining and cleaning the sacred things for such a holy place as the temple. All the same, we all have our families to consider, and a summons to go back to work over Passover was unheard of.

When we got there, and the crowd began to assemble in one of the bigger workshops, it soon became obvious that it was not all the craftsmen and women who had been summoned. There were no silversmiths or goldsmiths, for example, so it was clearly none of the metal items which needed repair. Come to think of it, there were no carpenters, either. In fact, when we looked around, there were only two groups. There were all the women who worked on the fabrics for the temple – stitching, embroidering and mending. Also, there was a small team of the labourers who did all the heavy lifting. Whatever was going on?

At a nod from the high priest, the team of labourers left the room and headed towards the inner court. Whilst they were gone, we all began to talk amongst ourselves, each new rumour clambering over the backs of the others to gain a hearing. By the time the doors opened again, there was quite a hubbub. All noise stopped dead, though, when the priests were followed back in by eight labourers, each group of four bearing their heavy burden. Once fully into the room, they carefully set their burden down and unfurled it. There were audible gasps as people saw that it was the temple curtain, torn into two almighty strips. In one corner, a group of the women who had worked here the longest began to sob as they saw the damage. Who, or what, could have done such a thing?

At first there was a hush as we set to work on this enormous repair. It was tough going, with the many layers which made up the heavy material. Of course, as the hours went by, people began to talk to those beside them. Apparently, this torn curtain was not the only strange thing this day. There had been darkness over the city in the middle of the day too, such as no one had ever seen. What everyone thought but no one spoke was this: did such things mean that God himself was cursing us or maybe blessing us? The answers lay outside this room...

● ● ● Pause to reflect

I have always thought of the moment that the temple curtain was ripped as one of supreme liberation, as the access to God was forced open. For those to whom it had been a symbol of God's majesty and holiness, it may have felt rather different.

Prayer

Dear God, how hard it can be sometimes to tell whether the unexpected event is you at work or not. Please help me to be better at telling the difference, I pray. Amen.

Act on it!

At this very moment there are people who would love to embrace the freedom and liberty offered by the gospel but feel that it overturns the traditions they have always held dear. Pray for them now.

Story 33

After the Banquet

> 'Now draw some out and take it to the master of the banquet.' They did so, and the master of the banquet tasted the water that had been turned into wine. He did not realise where it had come from, though the servants who had drawn the water knew. Then he called the bridegroom aside and said, 'Everyone brings out the choice wine first and then the cheaper wine after the guests have had too much to drink; but you have saved the best till now.'
>
> *(John 2:8–10)*

With a cheery wave and a promise to stay in touch, the last of the guests loaded up their belongings and headed for the open road. Many had travelled a long distance for the wedding, and the glow of its happiness and the sound of the singing would accompany them all the way home. Their hearts were full of happy memories, and their stomachs full of the best food and drink which their host could provide. Many would be discussing the wine as they travelled, especially. Unusually, it had got better rather than worse as the festivities had gone on. However had their host afforded that, they wondered?

Now the clearing up could start in earnest. The garlands came down first, and then the awnings that had protected the guests from the sun. The clay lamps that had lit the tables at night were carefully packed away, and any scraps of food set to one side for the goats. The clay goblets that had survived would be washed and used again, whilst those whose cracks were showing would go back into the earth from which they had been made. Most of the wine had gone, and the amphorae would also be washed to return to the merchant who had supplied them.

A servant who was going to tip out the last of the wine was stopped by a sharp cry from his master. At first he cowered, thinking he would be scolded for wastefulness, or worse still, accused of trying to steal it for himself. A look at his master's face assured him that all was well, though. He was striding towards him with a broad smile and a hand outstretched clutching an exquisite glass bottle. He told the servant to fill it with the wine that was left, and then inserted the stopper with an almost reverential concentration. He explained that he would keep it forever and pass it onto his children as a reminder that God, rather than he, was the great provider. As he turned away, bearing his prize, towards the house, the servant shook his head and smiled. If his master could remember such a thing, that would be a miracle indeed, he thought.

● ● ● Pause to reflect

This miracle would have been impressive even if the water was turned into reasonable wine. The fact that it was turned

After the Banquet

into the best wine, and that in large quantities, is a measure of the generosity of God.

Prayer

Dear God, today my prayer is a very simple one – that I might not forget all the good things you have done. Amen.

● ● ● Act on it!

This first miracle of Jesus was enacted in the unexpected context of a wedding celebration. Resolve today to look for the hand of God where you least expect it.

Story 34

Stargazing

> He came to Jesus at night and said, 'Rabbi, we know that you are a teacher who has come from God. For no one could perform the signs you are doing if God were not with him.' Jesus replied, 'Very truly I tell you, no one can see the kingdom of God unless they are born again.' 'How can someone be born when they are old?' Nicodemus asked. 'Surely they cannot enter a second time into their mother's womb to be born!' Jesus answered, 'Very truly I tell you, no one can enter the kingdom of God unless they are born of water and the Spirit. Flesh gives birth to flesh, but the Spirit gives birth to spirit. You should not be surprised at my saying, 'You must be born again.' The wind blows wherever it pleases. You hear its sound, but you cannot tell where it comes from or where it is going. So it is with everyone born of the Spirit.' 'How can this be?' Nicodemus asked.
>
> *(John 3:2-9)*

There comes a point in the later watches of the night when the only people left on the city's streets are those who look like they shouldn't be there. Some are hawking their wares, often their own bodies. Others have struck a deal away from prying eyes and are scuttling home to count up their winnings. Then there are those who have taken one cup of wine too many. They totter unsteadily from doorway to doorway as if on the deck of an unstable ship.

Something you hardly ever see is a religious man, which is why Nicodemus stood out. The plain brown cloak he had thrown over his robes was all very well, but it only had to slip to show who he truly was. I caught a glimpse of the finer clothes underneath – the expensive, richly dyed materials which only an important man could afford.

As he walked, he was shaking his head from side to side, as if to lose a thought which had clung there unwanted. Given how clever these men are, I would be surprised if any thought were so deep or complex to trouble that old grey head. Even so, his high forehead was deeply furrowed as if this pious man were torn to his very soul. As he passed me by, unseen in the shadows, I could have sworn I heard him praying under his breath. It was as if he had heard a truth so bizarre that he could not possibly find room for it in his ordered mind.

I followed him then, as he made his way out through the nearest gate and stood on a rise overlooking the valley below. Instead of looking at the graves of the great and the good down there in the valley, though, he turned his head upwards. This bookish man had turned his face to the stars as if he simply could not think where else to look for an answer to his question. Whatever had he heard back there, I wonder?

I hope he worked it out, I really do. Great men should have great peace, I think – or they become small and troubled, like the rest of us.

● ● ● **Pause to reflect**

Sometimes great learning and a towering intellect can make it harder to accept things that only faith can grasp.

What Happened Next?

When Nicodemus next appears in Scripture, it is obvious that he is thinking differently about Jesus (John 7:50–51).

Prayer

Dear God, today I pray for all those who are deeply troubled by the things you have to say to them. Bring comfort and clarity, and where they need a friend or counsellor, I pray that you would provide it. Amen.

● ● ● Act on it!

Being honest, what is the one claim in Scripture which you find hardest to accept? It is always good to talk to God about it, but seek out a Christian friend or leader with whom you can discuss it today.

Story 35

No Mat Today

> Now there is in Jerusalem near the Sheep Gate a pool, which in Aramaic is called Bethesda and which is surrounded by five covered colonnades. Here a great number of disabled people used to lie – the blind, the lame, the paralysed. One who was there had been an invalid for thirty-eight years. When Jesus saw him lying there and learned that he had been in this condition for a long time, he asked him, 'Do you want to get well?' 'Sir,' the invalid replied, 'I have no one to help me into the pool when the water is stirred. While I am trying to get in, someone else goes down ahead of me.' Then Jesus said to him, 'Get up! Pick up your mat and walk.' At once the man was cured; he picked up his mat and walked.
> *(John 5:2-9)*

For as long as he could remember, he had done this every day at sundown. During the day, it was for other people whose needs were far greater than his. From his house on the corner, he would watch them come as the city began to wake up. Some would hobble on homemade sticks – often as gnarled and bent as their owners. Others would lean on the arm of a friend, though often those friends grew weary of the daily routine and would come no longer.

There was one whom he knew as Reuben, though he was not sure of the name. His father had told him that Reuben had been coming day after day with a look of pitiful hope on his face. Every day, someone would deposit him under the colonnade on the eastern side of the pool, in exactly the same spot. He would lie there on his ragged bed with his chipped earthenware bowl by his side, in the hope that some might at least be generous to him at the spectacle of someone else's healing. Again and again and again he came back – to the extent that the flagstones in that eastern corner bore a sort of shiny imprint from his bed.

He could see it now, as he headed up that eastern colonnade with the last rays of the sun dividing it into geometric segments. In fact, the light seemed to light up Reuben's shiny spot like never before. Something caught his eye, though. Right there, beside the 'bed shadow' was Reuben's bowl – with a few mites and a shekel or two rattling around in the bottom of it. Whyever would he leave it behind, he wondered? Looking this way and that to make sure that no one was watching, he picked it up. After all, stealing a beggar's bowl would be the lowest form of crime. Instead, he took it home so that he could reunite Reuben with it the next day. After all, he knew exactly where to find him.

The thing is, Reuben never came. Day after day the man came back to look, bearing the bowl in his hands like some precious antique. As weeks turned to months and months turned to years, Reuben's shiny bed shadow faded away – scuffed and obscured by the passage of dusty feet.

And as for the bowl, he ended up adding to it so the little pile of coins inside grew and grew. One day he would give it to a bunch of Jesus' friends to help those in need, but that's another story.

● ● ● Pause to reflect

When I get to heaven, I really want to meet Reuben (or whatever his name might have been). I want to hear first-hand about the day that changed his life forever.

Prayer

Dear God, I pray for those who have waited long and hard for healing. Today, I stand with them in their perplexity and frustration, and ask that you would hear their prayers. Amen.

● ● ● Act on it!

If you find some money today, loose change in your purse or pockets, or unexpectedly in the back of a drawer or even on the pavement, take some time to think about where you might donate it in order to do some good for others.

Story 36

The Woman and the Sand

The teachers of the law and the Pharisees brought in a woman caught in adultery. They made her stand before the group and said to Jesus, 'Teacher, this woman was caught in the act of adultery. In the Law Moses commanded us to stone such women. Now what do you say?' They were using this question as a trap, in order to have a basis for accusing him. But Jesus bent down and started to write on the ground with his finger. When they kept on questioning him, he straightened up and said to them, 'Let any one of you who is without sin be the first to throw a stone at her.' Again he stooped down and wrote on the ground. At this, those who heard began to go away one at a time, the older ones first, until only Jesus was left, with the woman still standing there. Jesus straightened up and asked her, 'Woman, where are they? Has no one condemned you?' 'No one, sir,' she said. 'Then neither do I condemn you,' Jesus declared. 'Go now and leave your life of sin.'

(John 8:4–11)

The whole of that morning was a ghastly jumble in my head. A moment of warmth and intimacy suddenly became a circus act – with me as the gaudy fool. Those men had dragged me half-dressed from the house, hair uncovered like a common whore, and marched me through the streets for all to see. Some had frowns on their faces, but most had sickening grins, as if this were the best sport they had enjoyed for a long time.

The Woman and the Sand

As we rounded the last corner, there was a crowd already. I assumed they had been warned of what was to come and had come out to enjoy the prospect of a public shaming and the brutal end which would follow it. In fact, that was not why they were there. They had gathered at the street corner to listen to Jesus, the travelling teacher from Galilee. The men seemed to think this was even better sport and hurled me gleefully at his feet like a bunch of filthy rags.

Reading their minds, Jesus told them that whichever of them was sinless should feel free to cast the first stone that would bring about my end. After that, he turned his back on them, and bent down to write something in the sand on the roadside. I could see it clearly, since my head was turned, as I could not look anyone in the eye. Head bowed, like that, I waited for the first blow to fall – but nothing came. Often when you see little, you hear much, and I could hear one, then another, then another turn away and leave. In the end, when all were gone, Jesus straightened up and so did I. In one breath he cancelled the stench which had overtaken my life and sent me away to breathe freely and live cleanly. Those were the sweetest, kindest words that any man has ever spoken to me.

People often ask me if I saw what he wrote in the sand. I did. They also ask me if I will tell them, and I will not. It seems to me that he wrote those words only for an audience of one, and that *one* will carry them in her heart until her last breath.

What Happened Next?

● ● ● **Pause to reflect**

Jesus is the only person in this story to ask the woman a question, and thereby acknowledge that she has the right to be heard.

Prayer

Dear God, I want to thank you for the word of forgiveness which you have spoken over my life. I have done nothing to merit or deserve it, and yet you have granted it to me. Help me to live by it, I pray. Amen.

● ● ● **Act on it!**

Whenever I would naturally write 'men and women' or 'brothers and sisters', I deliberately write them the other way round. It is a tiny gesture, but it reminds me that for years we have placed women second in so very many ways. Why not give it a go?

Story 37

Fussed and Fuzzy

Then Jesus said, 'Did I not tell you that if you believe, you will see the glory of God?' So they took away the stone. Then Jesus looked up and said, 'Father, I thank you that you have heard me. I knew that you always hear me, but I said this for the benefit of the people standing here, that they may believe that you sent me.'

When he had said this, Jesus called in a loud voice, 'Lazarus, come out!' The dead man came out, his hands and feet wrapped with strips of linen, and a cloth round his face. Jesus said to them, 'Take off the grave clothes and let him go.'

(John 11:40–44)

As a brother to his two sisters, Lazarus had long ago perfected the art of being fussed over by those who loved him. Growing up, it seemed to him often that Mary and Martha would take it in turns to mother him, whilst their mother's back was turned. She was long gone, of course, and resting now with God. There was a thought somewhere in the back of his mind that he had left to join her. He had remembered a warm glow somewhere deep within at the prospect of it. Now it felt as if he had packed his bags and started on a journey, but somehow never left. The feeling was a dull one, coming from somewhere deep within. Nothing was quite clear, as if the past few days were wrapped in some kind of fog.

What Happened Next?

It was all hard to work out, since his thoughts, like his vision, were fuzzy. The nimble fingers of his sisters were plucking now at something wrapped all about his face. As they pulled it away, he felt a wave of familiarity and relief engulf him at the sight of their anxious faces. It was like playing their childhood games of 'little mums' all over again. But what were these wrappings he could see now on his arms and his legs? Why were they bound about his chest as if he were dressed for the grave? Panic rising now, he joined with Martha and Mary in their urgent hurry to tear them away. They felt dank and there was a smell about them which he could not bear.

At last the wrappings and bindings were off, in a small heap at his feet as though he had shed an unwanted garment. Still confused, and deeply disturbed, he noticed that his sisters were looking at him with tearful, yet joyful, faces. In fact, they were looking at him with a kind of urgent intensity as if they had thought they would never see him again. Whatever was going on? He shook his head as hard as he could, as if to dislodge the confusion within, but it didn't help. Opening his mouth to ask whatever had happened, he spotted another face over the shoulders of his smiling sisters. It was Jesus – a man who never seemed to be in the least bit troubled or confused. Maybe he would know what was going on?

● ● ● **Pause to reflect**

I sometimes wonder whether the whole of Lazarus' life from this point onwards felt like a second chance.

Prayer

Dear God, sometimes when I look around me, I feel as if I don't know what is really going on, deep down. I am not sure whether to rejoice, panic, or scratch my head in puzzlement. Set me straight today, I pray. Amen.

● ● ● **Act on it!**

Treat today, like all of Lazarus' extra ones, as an unexpected bonus, and see what happens . . .

Story 38

Freed but Not Free

> With this he went out again to the Jews gathered there and said, 'I find no basis for a charge against him. But it is your custom for me to release to you one prisoner at the time of the Passover. Do you want me to release "the king of the Jews"?' They shouted back, 'No, not him! Give us Barabbas!' Now Barabbas had taken part in an uprising.
>
> *(John 18:38–40)*

If you go to a certain quarter of Jerusalem, there is a man who will do just about anything to help you. His name is Barabbas, and he has the strength of an ox. Look carefully and you will see that he bears many a scar from his days as a rebel leader. There is an ugly wheal on his left cheek, some say from a short Roman sword. His ankles bear the marks from irons he has worn more than once. He never mentions these things, though. He will cheerfully carry your burden for you, or even pull your cart for a street or two if your donkey is lame. It seems like there is nothing that is too much trouble for him.

Those who know him well say it is as if every single day is a second chance for him. Meet him early in the morning, just as the rising sun peeps over the city walls, and you will find him shaking his head as if this were a miracle he never expected to see. By all accounts of his past, that would hardly be surprising. At sunset it is the same thing. Watching the sun sink over the horizon, his craggy face takes on a wistful expression, as if saying farewell to a day which had been a singular blessing.

Despite his positive outlook and his mighty strength, there is one place he will never ever go. He did it once by mistake. After offering to carry the load for a man who lived out beyond the city gates, they found themselves passing Golgotha. At the sight of it, this great mountain of a man put down his burden and sobbed like a small child. The man whom he was helping had to go on alone, and Barabbas stayed there until almost sundown – looking up at the hill and muttering again and again, 'It wasn't me.'

In the end, one or two of his neighbours came to guide him home. They said it was all something to do with his past, and a narrow escape from death. By the next morning, he was up with the sun again, greeting it like an old friend who had paid him a surprise visit. All the same, he never went out of the city that way again.

● ● ● Pause to reflect

The fact that forgiveness is free is one of the most joyful truths of the gospel. However, we must recognise that we often feel a deep desire to 'pay it back' in other ways.

Prayer

Dear God, it seems that very often I remember the things I would do better to forget, and forget the things I ought to remember. With your help, I long to be better at accepting the past and embracing the future, since both belong to you. Help me to do that, I pray. Amen.

Act on it!

Do you know a Barabbas, someone who can never seem to do enough for others because of what God has done for them? Make a point of thanking them for what they do today.

Story 39

A New Family

> When Jesus saw his mother there, and the disciple whom he loved standing near by, he said to her, 'Woman, here is your son,' and to the disciple, 'Here is your mother.' From that time on, this disciple took her into his home.
>
> *(John 19:26–27)*

At first, the two of them moved like automatons, each locked within their own wall-less cell of grief, shock and raw sadness. Mary had bowed her head and turned away from the cross just at the same moment as John. It was over now, and there was nothing to stay for in this wretched place. Without a word spoken between them, they had made their way through the streets towards Mary's house.

When they got there, she had sat by the door, hunched like a wounded animal as John gathered up her few possessions. Apart from the clothes she wore, a spare shawl and a few cooking pots, there was very little. John tucked all of that under one strong arm as he offered her the other to guide her to his house. Once again, no words were spoken, but she accepted the offer gladly enough.

Within a few hours, they began to speak a little – their voices still cracked from all the tears they had cried. They rehearsed the day's awful events, winced at the senseless cruelty of it all, and tried to mine for scraps of hope, like birds picking up the tiniest crumbs from the ground. It was not an easy task. They knew he would have wanted them to smile and not to fear – but neither could seem to see daylight above the lip of this pit into which they had been cast.

Of course, by the next day everything would change. Word would come from Mary Magdalene about her encounter in the garden, John would set off at a run to see if it were so and would come back home to tell Mary the glad news. After that, theirs became a happy, busy home. In the rare moments when there were no visitors, the two of them would share their memories of him and try to put his wonderful stories into their own words. It would be many months until it happened, but one day quite by accident he called her 'Mum' and never looked back. Like every other promise made by her remarkable Son – this one, uttered at the last, had also come true.

● ● ● Pause to reflect

In reading the Easter story, we are at a distinct disadvantage because we know the end from the beginning. Sometimes this prevents us from appreciating the real sorrow experienced by characters like John and Mary between the cross and the empty tomb.

A New Family

Prayer

Dear God, when I find myself in a new situation to which you have guided me, help me to find the scraps of hope as I wait to adjust. Amen.

● ● ● Act on it!

The word of Jesus bound Mary and John together like family. Is there someone who God has asked you to look out for with whom you need to be in touch?

Story 40

The Tale of a Tomb

Later, Joseph of Arimathea asked Pilate for the body of Jesus. Now Joseph was a disciple of Jesus, but secretly because he feared the Jewish leaders. With Pilate's permission, he came and took the body away. He was accompanied by Nicodemus, the man who earlier had visited Jesus at night. Nicodemus brought a mixture of myrrh and aloes, about thirty-five kilograms. Taking Jesus' body, the two of them wrapped it, with the spices, in strips of linen. This was in accordance with Jewish burial customs. At the place where Jesus was crucified, there was a garden, and in the garden a new tomb, in which no one had ever been laid. Because it was the Jewish day of Preparation and since the tomb was near by, they laid Jesus there.

(John 19:38–42)

There's a funeral going on in the Garden of Gethsemane today, and it has to be one of the strangest I have ever seen. The man they are burying is called Joseph, and in years gone by he was a member of the ruling council. His sort are generally as noisy in death as they were in life. They like to make their exit from this world as showy, pious and public as they possibly can. Many of them have their tomb hewn from the solid rock years before they die. It is a kind of morbid one-upmanship – showing every grieving family as they pass by that there are others more important than them. Rumour has it that this one once had such a tomb a little further into the garden.

The Tale of a Tomb

Apparently, he gave it away, long before his time had come. Back in the days of Pilate, he had some teacher by the name of Jesus buried there, as if it were his own kin. You can visit the tomb today, if you want. There's no marker of any kind, but you can pick it out a mile off because the stone door is rolled back and broken. No one will ever use that one again.

So instead, Joseph is being buried in this pauper's grave. There's quite a crowd of mourners there, quietly praying and singing hymns to the God they love. Surprisingly enough, there are smiles on many faces, as if they were almost rejoicing. You would have thought they were waving off a friend on the journey of a lifetime rather than grieving a loss. So very odd.

And do you know the oddest thing of all? The chief mourner is another public figure: Nicodemus the Pharisee, no less! Whatever would his religious friends think if they saw him now, standing at this pauper's grave and singing these folksy songs? This is hardly the behaviour expected of a Pharisee, of all people. He's either lost his grip, or found it – and doesn't care whatever else he loses in the process.

● ● ● Pause to reflect

Quite rightly, our thoughts at Easter turn to the emptied tomb. What about the empty tomb, though? In donating it, Joseph of Arimathea was demonstrating a public and dangerous commitment to Christ.

What Happened Next?

Prayer

Dear God, I long to be the kind of person who clings defiantly to hope, without worrying what other people think of me. Help me to take a step in that direction today. Amen.

● ● ● **Act on it!**

If God called on you today to give away something precious, could you do it? Think about it, and perhaps discuss it with a trusted Christian friend.

Story 41

A Garden Walk

> Thinking he was the gardener, she said, 'Sir, if you have carried him away, tell me where you have put him, and I will get him.' Jesus said to her, 'Mary.' She turned toward him and cried out in Aramaic, 'Rabboni!' (which means 'Teacher'). Jesus said, 'Do not hold on to me, for I have not yet ascended to the Father. Go instead to my brothers and tell them, "I am ascending to my Father and your Father, to my God and your God."'
>
> *(John 20:15–17)*

. . . and with that, all sight and sound of him was gone. Every created thing seemed more alive, though. Each droplet of dew seemed bursting as if it reflected the whole of God's heaven above, rather than just a glimpse. The birds threw back their heads and gulped great lungfuls of air to sing out louder than they had ever done. The rustling, silver-green branches of the olive trees seemed to swish in unison, as if some great being had just brushed fingertips through them on his way out of the garden.

Out! That was where she was supposed to be going. Just one second before, she had been a woman bowed beneath the weight of her sorrow. In the next, she had been a worshipper, falling towards the feet of her Lord as if she would never let them go. Before she could reach them, she was told not to touch but to see, to believe and then to go and tell what she had seen. Now she was a witness to the reversal of heaven's laws and the very heartbeat of the earth. She had seen the impossible and knew it to be true. Like the songbirds with their extra-loud song, she wanted to throw back her head and shout that the world was different now.

Once out of the garden her pace would quicken, and she would make a list in her head of all the people she should tell as she ran to find them. As she went, she would try to formulate the sentences which would make some sense of this gloriously senseless thing. Not yet, though. Not until she reached the garden's edge would the hurry begin. For now, she bent and carefully removed her sandals that she might feel the swish of the damp grass on the soles of her feet. Every pace was like a first step in a brand-new world, and she wanted to savour them all.

● ● ● Pause to reflect

To us now, the resurrection is a very public event, celebrated by every church and denomination across the world. This encounter with Jesus was intensely personal for Mary, though, just as her first had been.

A Garden Walk

Prayer

Dear God, today I pray for the eyes to see how new the world truly is in the light of your resurrection. With each step, may I be aware that I am treading on hallowed ground, made special by you. Amen.

● ● ● **Act on it!**

Take a pen (or find a keyboard!) and start to write down all the things which are different because of the resurrection.

Story 42

A Netful of Fish

> He said, 'Throw your net on the right side of the boat and you will find some.' When they did, they were unable to haul the net in because of the large number of fish. Then the disciple whom Jesus loved said to Peter, 'It is the Lord!' As soon as Simon Peter heard him say, 'It is the Lord,' he wrapped his outer garment around him (for he had taken it off) and jumped into the water. The other disciples followed in the boat, towing the net full of fish, for they were not far from shore, about a hundred metres. When they landed, they saw a fire of burning coals there with fish on it, and some bread. Jesus said to them, 'Bring some of the fish you have just caught.' So Simon Peter climbed back into the boat and dragged the net ashore. It was full of large fish, 153, but even with so many the net was not torn.
>
> *(John 21:6–11)*

Have you ever walked down from the hills and smelt the woodsmoke even before you could see the houses of the village? Or maybe you have walked into a place just as dusk falls and the cooking fires are lit? With a sensitive nose you can pick out the different scents – meat, herbs, smoke and maybe even the sharp tang of olives. On this particular occasion, it was not the mixture of smells which would have struck you. Rather, it was the fact that the same smell was coming from every direction – fish, fish and more fish. Of course that was not unusual on the shores of the lake, but this was on another level entirely. It was as if the entire fish population of the lake had decided to present themselves at the net.

A Netful of Fish

For those who had worked the lake that previous night, it had been a fruitless one. It was like that sometimes – either the fish were scared, or the boat was in the wrong place. Not this time, though. Early in the morning the cry had gone up that something miraculous had happened down on the shore – and everybody had rushed down to look. Sure enough, there was a haul of fish the like of which nobody had ever seen. The net was pushed to its very limits with its glistening harvest from the waters. Of course, it was far too much for any one family to use, and the men who had caught it seemed busy with someone else further up the beach. So, one or two started passing them – one here and two there until all were gone. It was not entirely haphazard, though, as there was a man jotting down the numbers as they passed them out.

As the last fish found its way into a grateful pair of hands, he stood and pronounced the number 153 to no one in particular. When the nearest person looked startled, he explained, 'I shall write this down one day – you just wait and see.' I wonder if he ever did?

● ● ● Pause to reflect

The fact that the disciples had gone out fishing at all was symptomatic of their dejection and their return to life as it had been before Jesus. With their hopes dashed (as they had thought), it was all they knew.

What Happened Next?

Prayer

Dear God, today I pray for a delicious opportunity to share some of your good things. I want not just to enjoy them, but to enjoy sharing them. Amen.

● ● ● **Act on it!**

Count out 153 of something on a table – whether it be coins, toy bricks, or pieces of pasta. You will find that it makes for quite a heap – and stands as a reminder of the enormity of this miracle.

Story 43

Onwards and Upwards

> After he said this, he was taken up before their very eyes, and a cloud hid him from their sight. They were looking intently up into the sky as he was going, when suddenly two men dressed in white stood beside them. 'Men of Galilee,' they said, 'why do you stand here looking into the sky? This same Jesus, who has been taken from you into heaven, will come back in the same way you have seen him go into heaven.' Then the apostles returned to Jerusalem . . .
>
> *(Acts 1:9–12)*

One week ago, the sudden appearance of two angels would have shaken these men to the core. After everything which had happened in-between, it scarcely registered. They had lived through more emotions in this past week than at any other point in their lives. There had been the elation of coming into the city like acolytes to a conquering hero, riding on the wave of cheers from the crowds. After that had come the shock and fear as Jesus trashed the temple and they flinched in anticipation of the consequences. They had shared the strangest of meals with him on Passover night, looking down at the top of his crownless head as he had knelt to wash their feet. None had understood his disturbing words about broken bodies and poured-out blood. After that had come the garden, the torches, the arrest and Jesus led away trussed-up like a prize stag for a king's table.

What Happened Next?

No one even wanted to think about the Friday, with its nails and its midday blackness. And then, he was back. And now, he was gone.

'He will come back' came the clarion voice of the angels, interrupting their thoughts. With that, they turned and headed back down the hill towards Jerusalem. There was no clear plan in their minds, just that they felt drawn towards it as the epicentre of where it had all happened. It took half the journey until any of them felt able to speak, as if the sound of their voices would somehow break the spell of what they had seen and heard.

'You know when he said we would be witnesses,' said the youngest, and they all nodded. 'And he said it would be in Jerusalem and Judea and Samaria?' Once again, they all nodded their assent. 'Where was it after that?' Nobody dared speak at that point. All stopped on the road, half way between the hills and the city, and looked to John. They usually left the harder things to him to say. The colour drained from his familiar face as he reminded them that the instruction had talked about the earth's furthest reaches. None of them had ever been beyond Samaria . . .

● ● ● Pause to reflect

Many artists have struggled to depict this moment, and medieval paintings with the feet of Jesus disappearing into a cloud tend to make us smile. However, the sense of abandonment and apprehension for the disciples would have been palpable.

Prayer

Dear God, please give courage to those today who cross borders and go to unfamiliar places to share your word. In those unfamiliar places, may you be their strength and guide. Amen.

Act on it!

Take a piece of paper and draw five circles inside each other. Write your name in the centre circle. In the next one, write the names of your family. In the next one out, write the names of your close friends. In the one beyond that, write the names of your neighbours, and in the one beyond that the names of any colleagues you might have. Congratulations – you have just drawn a picture of your mission field!

Story 44

A Trail of Footprints

> With many other words he warned them; and he pleaded with them, 'Save yourselves from this corrupt generation.' Those who accepted his message were baptised, and about three thousand were added to their number that day.
>
> *(Acts 2:40–41)*

Wet footprints on dusty roads are gone in a flash, like the last shreds of morning mist when the sun breaks through. Perhaps if there were two or three, they might last a little longer, but not by much. What about if there were 100, though? What about if the 100 were 1,000, and the 1,000 were 3,000? On that day the crowd had moved as one seething mass from the outskirts of the temple to the pool at the city's edge. For hour upon hour they had gone into the water one by one to proclaim their allegiance to Jesus. 'Jesus is Lord!' went up the cry again and again, as this one and that plunged momentarily under the water. The air itself seemed to shudder with joy as each new life was declared.

As each had risen from the water and clambered out of the pool, so they had brought some of its contents with them. It ran down off their hair, made their glad faces shine, and dripped from the hems of their clothing. In the end, it started to form a small river down the centre of the street. By the time evening came, the water level had fallen so low that many had to crouch down to feel the cooling water embrace them from top to toe. No one seemed to mind, though, either amongst those who clambered in or those who waited their turn.

When the last of them climbed out, he was followed by Peter and his eleven friends. All were tired, and their shoulders ached after the many hours of bending and lifting each new sister and brother into the water and then out. None of them were strangers to the water, but they seemed jubilant about it now. All the way down the muddy river that had now formed in the road, they splashed and danced and laughed like children gleefully jumping in puddles. Despite the setting sun, it felt more like the beginning of a new day than its end.

Pause to reflect

There must have been a lot of waiting around on that day, as 3,000 people all waited their turn to get baptised. Had I been there, I wonder whether I would have held my nerve until I got to the head of the queue?

Prayer

Dear God, I thank you for the courage of those who declare their faith in Jesus publicly for all to see. Keep the joy in their hearts as their journey of faith unfolds, wherever it may take them, I pray. Amen.

● ● ● Act on it!

Think of someone known to you who has taken a great step of faith recently. Shut your eyes and picture their face, and then take a moment to share *their* joy as you pray for them.

Story 45

A Change of Fortune

> Once when we were going to the place of prayer, we were met by a female slave who had a spirit by which she predicted the future. She earned a great deal of money for her owners by fortune-telling. She followed Paul and the rest of us, shouting, 'These men are servants of the Most High God, who are telling you the way to be saved.' She kept this up for many days. Finally Paul became so annoyed that he turned round and said to the spirit, 'In the name of Jesus Christ I command you to come out of her!' At that moment the spirit left her.
>
> *(Acts 16:16–18)*

Today was the day when Julia would be twice free, though she did not know it at the time. The day had started like any other, with her master escorting her to the busiest markets like an exotic pet. She was not chained, as that would have been bad for business, but she may as well have been. She was utterly dependent on him for her meagre food and lodging, and he was the only thing between her and a life of mad ravings amongst the tombstones or on the road out of town. As per usual, he would pick his client, extol her prescient virtues to him, agree a fee, and then Julia would circle the victim moaning and snarling before sliding into clearer speech and declaring their fortune in a monotone.

On this occasion, she broke away from her master and followed two strangers down the road. With them, she was more certain than she had ever been that God was present.

What Happened Next?

The voice in her head was so loud that she had to scream and shout to all who would hear that these two were on a mission from God. She had done this for two days already and been beaten on both occasions. Free declarations don't make money. The third time it happened, her master looked as if he would beat her within an inch of her life if she dared to speak up. In fact, she did not need to. Paul, one of the men, spun around and banished the demon who gave her the second sight. Instantly she felt different, as if simultaneously deflated and elated. Her master dismissed her on the spot, declaring that she was of no use to him like this, and went off in pursuit of Paul.

Confused, delighted and feeling slightly drunk with freedom, Julia stumbled down the road with no idea of where she would go. Somebody did, though. Not long after that, she bumped into a kindly woman named Lydia, who said that she could stay with her that night. It turns out that she had not seen the last of Paul . . .

● ● ● **Pause to reflect**

If the description of this woman having 'owners' does not make us shudder, then it should. Thank God that she met up with Paul and the others, so that she could be truly free.

Prayer

Dear God, today I pray for all who are trapped. Whether it is habit, circumstance or history that imprisons them, I ask you to set them free. Amen.

● ● ● Act on it!

Find the name today of a Christian agency working to set people free from modern slavery of all kinds, such as Hope for Justice – https://hopeforjustice.org/. Pray for them and contact them to say that you are doing so.

Story 46

The Jail Menders

> About midnight Paul and Silas were praying and singing hymns to God, and the other prisoners were listening to them. Suddenly there was such a violent earthquake that the foundations of the prison were shaken. At once all the prison doors flew open, and everyone's chains came loose. The jailer woke up, and when he saw the prison doors open, he drew his sword and was about to kill himself because he thought the prisoners had escaped. But Paul shouted, 'Don't harm yourself! We are all here!' The jailer called for lights, rushed in and fell trembling before Paul and Silas. He then brought them out and asked, 'Sirs, what must I do to be saved?' They replied, 'Believe in the Lord Jesus, and you will be saved – you and your household.' Then they spoke the word of the Lord to him and to all the others in his house. At that hour of the night the jailer took them and washed their wounds; then immediately he and all his household were baptised.
>
> *(Acts 16:25-33)*

'A job's a job's a job, son,' my dad would say. 'You should only ask two questions, ever: what needs doing and who's paying for it, nothing else.' I knew those were the rules, but they had never been harder to obey.

Our customer this time was a funny sort – a jailer. Now, any jailer I have ever met has had a face like thunder and a temper like an angry camel. Not this one. He was friendly and obliging and happy to see us there. He kept muttering something about 'such an unforgettable night' under his breath as he showed us from one cell to the next. Why would a jailer be happy, I wondered, when someone had trashed his jail? Not only that, but *how* had they trashed it?

Every door was still firmly on its hinges, but the lock was broken clean in two. There were no saw-marks from cutting nor burrs where a tool might have twisted them. The manacles were the same. Each set was still firmly fixed to the wall, but each cuff was sliced down the middle, like a piece of cheese sliced with a wire. I had never seen anything like it. The prisoners in each cell smiled and nodded as we worked our way from cell to cell. To see their faces, you would have thought they'd had a party the previous night. They chatted and passed the time of day with the workmen, but nobody would say what had happened. It was as if they shared a guilty, joyous secret.

Generally, I never want to go back and visit a job again. After all, if you have to go back it's because you didn't do it well enough in the first place. All the same, I find myself stopping and staring every time I go past the jail. Whatever went on in there, I wonder?

● ● ● Pause to reflect

Had I been in that prison, I am not sure that midnight would have found me praying and singing to God. What about you?

What Happened Next?

> **Prayer**

Dear God, I sometimes feel I have got far too accustomed to stories of the miraculous things you can do. Take me by surprise today, I pray. Amen.

● ● ● Act on it!

If you are honest, what is the one prayer which it seems most impossible for God to answer? Could you be brave enough to share that need with someone today, and pray with faith for it together?

Story 47

Officially Awkward

> When it was daylight, the magistrates sent their officers to the jailer with the order: 'Release those men.' The jailer told Paul, 'The magistrates have ordered that you and Silas be released. Now you can leave. Go in peace.' But Paul said to the officers: 'They beat us publicly without a trial, even though we are Roman citizens, and threw us into prison. And now do they want to get rid of us quietly? No! Let them come themselves and escort us out.'
>
> *(Acts 16:35-37)*

There are some creatures, like owls and badgers, that are rarely seen in daylight. Amongst them would be the city's magistrates. These are powerful men who hold liberty, and even life, in their hands. In part they maintain their regime of fear by hiding themselves behind walls and underlings. If you actually get to see them, then you know that you are in trouble straight away. The one exception would be those occasions when the great and good parade through the city in all their finery wanting to be seen. This was not such a day.

They came in the milky light of an early dawn, constantly looking over their shoulders as if afraid of being spotted. These men who could strike fear into the heart with a haughty stare or some icy words seemed genuinely afraid now. They made their way to the back door so as to avoid prying eyes.

What Happened Next?

It was already too late for that, though. Such men as these cannot walk through the streets in such a posse and not expect to be seen. As they disappeared through the door, hustled in by the jailer, there was already a crowd gathering on the street corner.

By the time they came out, the growing crowd could see that they had two men with them. Both of these men bore the scuffs and bloodstains of the previous day's beatings on their clothing. Their faces were clean, though, and they looked to have been well fed. Oddly, although their injuries meant that both men walked gingerly, they had their heads held high. Whilst they smiled and nodded to onlookers in the crowd, the magistrates turned their heads away and stared at the ground, as if hoping that it might swallow them up and put an end to all this.

At the end of the street, the party stopped, and the magistrates pointed left towards the city gates, gesticulating as if they were desperate for the men to leave. After that, they all went their separate ways, as if hoping they would attract less attention as individuals. The two beaten men turned away from the city gate and headed towards the house of Lydia instead, to which many of the crowd followed them. Before night fell, the story of an angel's visit and a broken prison door would be told again and again.

● ● ● Pause to reflect

Why was it not sufficient that Paul and Silas should be released? Why do you think Paul insisted on an official escort?

Prayer

Dear God, today I pray for those imprisoned for their faith. If their stories will not end in liberation this day, then I ask you to stand right by their side. Amen.

● ● ● Act on it!

Some of the Christian agencies who work with people imprisoned for their faith can provide you with postal addresses so that you can write to your sisters and brothers in prison to encourage them. Why not have a go? For example, see Open Doors – www.opendoorsuk.org/act/letter/.

Story 48

A New Trade

> About that time there arose a great disturbance about the Way. A silversmith named Demetrius, who made silver shrines of Artemis, brought in a lot of business for the craftsmen there. He called them together, along with the workers in related trades, and said: 'You know, my friends, that we receive a good income from this business. And you see and hear how this fellow Paul has convinced and led astray large numbers of people here in Ephesus and in practically the whole province of Asia. He says that gods made by human hands are no gods at all. There is danger not only that our trade will lose its good name, but also that the temple of the great goddess Artemis will be discredited; and the goddess herself, who is worshipped throughout the province of Asia and the world, will be robbed of her divine majesty.' When they heard this, they were furious and began shouting: 'Great is Artemis of the Ephesians!'
>
> *(Acts 19:23–28)*

If you wanted to buy a souvenir in Ephesus, then you had only to head to the *agora*, in the city centre. It was meeting place, market square and parade ground all rolled into one. Of course, like everywhere else in Ephesus, it stood in the shadow of the great temple of Artemis, soaring into the sky with the gold glinting from the gaps between the bricks. This was the best place for the souvenir hunter – there were shops and kiosks all around the edge, and often temporary market stalls in the middle. At one or two of the shops, you could see through from the counter to the workshop behind, and sometimes watch the silversmith as he poured and then worked the molten metal.

Demetrius' shop had been just such a one. It still is now. Above the door it reads: 'Demetrius and son: silversmiths and jewellers by appointment'. If you ask him about the 'by appointment' bit he will be very cagey about answering you. He will wait until you are the only customer, and even then he will check up and down the street both ways before he dares to tell. All the same, it is not hard to see how his allegiances have changed. On the counter now are rows and rows of silver crosses – great and small. There are one or two fish symbols, too, their curving lines crossed at the tail as if ready to wiggle and swim at any moment. Rumour has it that there are still one or two of the old Artemis statuettes under the counter, but he rarely brings them out.

Soon his son will be running the shop instead of him, as Demetrius' hands tremble now when he pours the liquid silver, and his eyes are not as good as they were for fine work. When his son takes over, those last statuettes will go, you can be sure. Paul will have nothing to do with them.

● ● ● Pause to reflect

There are many places around the world where a decision to follow Christ means that people can no longer hold the jobs they once had.

What Happened Next?

Prayer

Dear God, to make a change and stand out against the culture all around you takes huge courage. Today, I pray for my Christian sisters and brothers who do it every single day. Amen.

● ● ● **Act on it!**

Next time you are buying a gift for someone, see if you can choose one which benefits a Christian trader or craftsman in a part of the world where their allegiance to Christ costs them financially.

Story 49

The Careless Listener

> On the first day of the week we came together to break bread. Paul spoke to the people and, because he intended to leave the next day, kept on talking until midnight. There were many lamps in the upstairs room where we were meeting. Seated in a window was a young man named Eutychus, who was sinking into a deep sleep as Paul talked on and on. When he was sound asleep, he fell to the ground from the third storey and was picked up dead. Paul went down, threw himself on the young man and put his arms round him. 'Don't be alarmed,' he said. 'He's alive!'
>
> *(Acts 20:7-10)*

I always loved to hear Paul speak. I would have walked until my feet bled just to be there and hear his words. Like many others, I had heard tales of the Messiah – all about his wonderful stories and the miracles he performed. Blind men saw, lame men leapt and danced, and apparently even the dead walked and talked at his command. Men like me had missed their chance, though. We had been in the wrong places to see these things for ourselves. Instead, we saw the power of Jesus reflected in the lives of those whom he had changed. In their voices and through their actions we saw his power to transform even the most twisted lives, and so we became his followers – Jesus people, if you like.

On that night people had started coming to the house even before Paul arrived to speak. There was an excited chatter as people swapped stories of what they had heard and seen. It was my own fault, really. I had wanted to stay outside until the last minute so that I could see him arrive for myself and greet him if I could. Of course, he did not know me, but it felt important. By the time that was done, and I went up the stairs, the place was full. There were people from wall to wall, their excited faces reflected in the lights of the candles burning in niches at the sides. My only hope was to pick my way across the room, avoiding laps and leaning on affable heads until I reached the window ledge. I pushed my back into the corner, drew my legs up so they were in no one's way, and listened with rapt attention as Paul started to speak.

The last thing I remember was an irritation with myself as my eyelids fell shut after a long, long day at work, and the candlelight made the room feel so warm and cosy. The next thing I knew, I was lying in the street outside, surrounded by pale, anxious faces, and the apostle himself was stretching a hand out to me and telling me to 'get up, brother'. I started to mumble something about how I had not meant to fall asleep, but he was already striding indoors, like a man on a mission. When I got back inside, I found that people had left me a space on the floor at the front, and a burly fisherman was stood blocking the window seat – arms folded and a big grin on his face.

Funnily enough, I'm the preacher now. I tell stories of the power of Jesus – but I always make sure that everyone is seated safely before I begin!

The Careless Listener

● ● ● **Pause to reflect**

If you had been there on that night, I wonder what you would have remembered most – the sermon or the event that interrupted it?

Prayer

Dear God, I pray today for all who will preach the gospel in churches and all kinds of other places too. May their hearts be full of courage and their words be full of grace. Amen.

● ● ● **Act on it!**

Next time you are listening to a sermon, try to do so *actively*. Take an exercise book or journal, if possible, and make a physical note of what it is about and what you should do as a consequence.

Story 50

Sandy Knees and Heavy Hearts

'In everything I did, I showed you that by this kind of hard work we must help the weak, remembering the words the Lord Jesus himself said: "It is more blessed to give than to receive." When Paul had finished speaking, he knelt down with all of them and prayed. They all wept as they embraced him and kissed him. What grieved them most was his statement that they would never see his face again. Then they accompanied him to the ship.

(Acts 20:35–38)

As the ship grew smaller in the distance, no one seemed to want to be the first to break eye contact with its sail. In part, this was because that ever-shrinking sail took with it a man who had been like an elder brother, father and friend. He had coaxed them and coached them, berated them and blessed them, and now they would never see him again. These words had been his last to them, and already they were trying to remember all the things he had said about his preaching and service and the task which lay before them. The other reason that no one wanted to look away was because they feared that the others might see the tears glistening on their cheeks. In fact, they need not have worried, since every face was the same. These men were neither fearful nor weak, and all led the church in a city where the air itself reeked of magic, and loyalty to Jesus cost everybody dear. They had best get used to seeing each other this way, as there would doubtless be more tears to be shed.

In the end, the sail was no more than a dot on the horizon, and by some unspoken consent, they all turned their backs on the sea. Ahead lay the road to Miletus, and beyond that the long road back home to Ephesus. The walk would take them many hours and there would be plenty of time to reflect along the way. None of them seemed to notice that they had sand on the edges of their clothes where they had knelt and prayed so hard. Even when they did, no one felt inclined to brush it off. In fact, it would go on to follow them around for days, like rice or confetti left over from a wedding and popping up when least expected. Those little grains would become blessed irritants – reminders of the mantle which now was theirs.

As they walked, the phrase to which they returned again and again was Jesus' words that it was 'more blessed to give than to receive'. Could that really be, they wondered? Could it really be that this man who had now left them had been more blessed by giving to them than he ever might have been by receiving from them? One day, when the city of Ephesus would be behind them and the New Jerusalem ahead of them, when the whole journey was done and every grain of sand had fallen from feet and clothes, they would ask him. One day . . .

What Happened Next?

● ● ● Pause to reflect

What do you think was the greatest reason for their tears as they stood with Paul on the beach?

Prayer

Dear God, I pray today for those who carry the burden of church leadership, doing their best to serve faithfully and well. Bless them, I pray. Amen.

● ● ● Act on it!

Write a card or email or send a text to a church leader today to thank them for their service and to assure them of your prayers.

Story 51

On the Beach

> Once safely on shore, we found out that the island was called Malta. The islanders showed us unusual kindness. They built a fire and welcomed us all because it was raining and cold. Paul gathered a pile of brushwood and, as he put it on the fire, a viper, driven out by the heat, fastened itself on his hand. When the islanders saw the snake hanging from his hand, they said to each other, 'This man must be a murderer; for though he escaped from the sea, the goddess Justice has not allowed him to live.' But Paul shook the snake off into the fire and suffered no ill effects.
> *(Acts 28:1–5)*

It must have been quite some fire on the beach last night. Even in the rain the flames had leapt high up into the air, and the glow went on long after the beach was empty. In the quiet of the next morning, I picked my way down there to see what was left behind. The most obvious thing was the prow of a prison ship, wedged between the rocks like some sea creature sniffing the spray which splashed up all around it. Behind it, floating on the waves, was a smattering of broken timber, as if the creature were thrashing its tail from side to side. Other pieces of timber were washed up in a line looking like someone had ridden them ashore. Scattered around were shreds of clothing and a rope or two.

On closer inspection, much of the fire had been made from broken timbers of the ship. Here and there a curved, charred beam jutted up into the morning sky. The rest of the fire seemed to have been made of driftwood, which had all burnt away to ash. Hanging on one resistant branch was the strangest thing – the remains of a viper. These unexpected visitors had surely not been trying to cook it, had they? Prisoners or not, I hope my fellow islanders had welcomed the poor wretches better than that. Reflecting on this, I started to follow the trail of footprints up and off the beach towards the governor's residence.

Part way there, I found myself in company. Beside me were many I recognised and others I did not. Some were limping or leaning on the arm of a friend. At least one was borne on a bier of some kind, as if too sick to rise. All were heading towards the governor's house as if drawn there by some inexorable hope. Apparently, one of the prisoners had not only shaken off a snake and lived, but his prayers could heal the sick. This was something I had to see, so I joined in with the crowd . . .

● ● ● Pause to reflect

Not surprisingly, Luke's account of this episode in the book of Acts focuses on Paul, but what became of all the other prisoners on that boat?

Prayer

Dear God, today I pray for all who will serve you by working with people who are in prison. Give them a length of patience and a depth of grace that they might truly speak and act for you, I pray. Amen.

● ● ● Act on it!

If you read on in Luke's story, you will find that Paul received a warm welcome on the island. Who could you welcome today, even if it is only for a cup of coffee and a bit of conversation?

Story 52

Full Stop

> He who testifies to these things says, 'Yes, I am coming soon.' Amen. Come, Lord Jesus. The grace of the Lord Jesus be with God's people. Amen.
>
> *(Rev. 22:20–21)*

With a sigh, the ageing prisoner put down his pen and shook the stiffness out of his wrist. At his feet lay the sheets of papyrus with words on them that he scarcely understood. Looking up, he was disappointed to see that the flaming vision so bright that it had eclipsed the noonday sun was no more. Its voice, like the voice of many trumpets, had been replaced now by the quiet conversation of his fellow prisoners and the keening of a seabird far overhead. Were it not for the papyri and their words, he would have thought it all a product of his tired and imprisoned imagination, but it was not so, he knew.

Deep down, despite the flames and the golden sash and the sword, he had known the voice that spoke. It was a voice he had heard on mountaintops and at the bedside of the sick. He had heard that voice tell stories, banish demons, bless children and berate the self-satisfied. It was the voice of Jesus: friend, Lord and constant companion, even now. He closed his eyes for a moment and thought of his friend's face: gazing down with love at a little child's head, laughing as his fishing friends hauled in the catch of their lives, crying beneath a crown of thorns. He shook that last one away, as it was too painful to bear. And now, it seemed, he could still hear that voice and still see that face, even after many years.

Wistfully, John looked out across the sea towards the mainland. He wondered how the other Jesus-followers were doing. He knew the names of only a few, but they felt like family to him nonetheless. They were his brothers and sisters, his nephews and nieces, adopted like him into the family of heaven. How he longed to see them and to hear their voices. What wouldn't he give right now to nod at the wisdom of the old ones and smile at the optimism of the young . . . If only he could be with them. On his darker days he feared that they might not stay the course, that they might feel somehow as if they had risked too much on the words of Jesus. What they needed to know was that the end was good and sure, no matter what came between now and then. Who could tell them? Looking down at the papyri he had filled, and across at a guard preparing to sail to the mainland, John had an idea . . .

● ● ● Pause to reflect

For John, the eyes of faith allowed him to see beyond his immediate circumstances to God's bigger picture. It is a skill we all need.

Prayer

Dear God, thank you for all the inspiration and comfort that is in your revealed word. I thank you for those who wrote it down, and for others who have translated it that I might read it today. Amen.

● ● ● Act on it!

If you have never done so before, read the preface to your Bible today, since it tells you all about the work which went into translating it.

What Happens Next?

I hope you have enjoyed these little stories. I hope they have made you think, laugh and even cry. In all that you have read, the intention has never been to *add* to Scripture, but rather to make you look at it that little bit harder and feel it that little bit deeper. When I was growing up, I used to love to buy Action Transfer sets from the toy shop. Each came equipped with an exciting, dramatic background such as a fantasy cave or a battle scene. Also in the packet was a set of transfers, a sheet of greaseproof paper and a short pencil. To get started all you had to do was select the relevant transfer, place it where you thought it belonged on the scene, place the greaseproof paper over it, and then rub hard with the pencil. After that came the magical moment where you peeled back the transfer sheet to reveal your little transfer helping to bring the bigger scene to life. All of a sudden, this was *your* story rather than a blank scene. You could put the pirates or dragons or soldiers wherever you thought they needed to be to depict the story.

I hope that you will find some pages of the Bible now feel that way. Maybe next time you read the Bible passages themselves you will find yourselves looking out for an Anna or a Barabbas or a Reuben lurking somewhere on the edge of the crowd. Maybe you will end up asking yourself how it felt to see the ripped curtain taken down in the temple, or see a dead man climb down off his bier. To engage with the pages of Scripture in this imaginative way can only help our reading of it.

Having read these fifty-two stories, why not start hunting in the Bible for other stories whose consequences or 'unfinished endings' are unknown to us? There will be hundreds, from Rahab emerging from the ruins of Jericho to every sick or needy person touched by Jesus. Each time you read a Bible story, keep your eyes peeled for the people who would have been immediately affected by what was going on. They might be adults or children, famous people or unknowns – but all are touched by the works of God. You could even think about some of the people whom Jesus sent away with a flea in their ear for their unbelief or their foolish questions. How might *their* stories have continued?

As an alternative, you could take another look at *these* fifty-two stories, and consider how they might have continued. You might think that the way I have imagined them is far wide of the mark and have a much better version of your own. You might see sadness where I have seen joy, or faith where I have seen doubt. The excitement of doing this is that it can easily come out differently every time.

On my landing window I have a glass sculpture. It is a misshapen bowl, looking as if it is dripping down the forked tree branch that holds it. Inside are hundreds of brightly coloured, reflective stars – the kind of thing you get inside party poppers. On a bright day, these stars throw up little patches of coloured light onto the walls and the ceiling all around. The patches are in different places every time, depending on the position of the sun. The stars themselves are always the same, and the bowl which holds them is always the same – it is only the reflections that change. Even so, our reflections on any given story in the Bible may change from time to time, though the story itself remains the same.

I believe that God is still writing stories just like these, and he is doing it in the lives of the people reading this book. After all that he had seen of the work of God through Christ in a relatively short space of time, John could not believe that the stories were over. In fact, he stated at the end of his gospel that God was still writing them:

> **Jesus did many other things as well. If every one of them were written down, I suppose that even the whole world would not have room for the books that would be written.**
>
> ***(John 21:25)***

As we draw to a close, let's come back to a word used in the first chapter of this book. Every time God's story *collides* with ours, a new story begins. Like one atom colliding with another, it causes a release of energy, and something new is forged. To look at it another way, it is like a woodcarver's chisel striking the bare wood, that a new shape might be born out of it. In this way we are shaped and shaped and shaped again

What Happened Next?

by the carpenter of Nazareth. As I reflect on that, it makes me wonder whether we should get more into the habit of writing down our faith stories, so that we can reflect on what God is doing with us? Maybe that is a subject for another book. Maybe that is *what happens next* for me.

What about you?

Bibliography

Augustine, *Confessions* (New York: HarperPress, 2021)

Brueggemann, W. *Hopeful Imagination: Prophetic Voices in Exile* (Philadelphia, PA: Fortress Press, 1986)

From Our Own Correspondent: A Celebration of Fifty Years of the BBC Radio Programme (ed. Tony Grant; London: Profile Books, 2005)

Littledale, R. *Stale Bread: A Handbook for Speaking the Story* (Edinburgh: Saint Andrew Press, 2011)

Mwamba, T. *Dancing Sermons* (London: SPCK, 2007)

Schlafer, D. *Playing with Fire: Preaching Work as Kindling Art* (Cowley Publications: Cambridge, MA, 2004)

Smith, D. *Disney A to Z: The Official Encyclopedia* (Westport, CT: Hyperion, 1996)

Troeger, Thomas H. *Imagining a Sermon* (Nashville, TN: Abingdon Press, 1990)

End Notes

Chapter 1

[1] Dave Smith, *Disney A to Z: The Official Encyclopedia* (Westport, CT: Hyperion, 1996).

[2] Augustine, *Confessions* (New York: HarperPress, 2021), Book 11, Chapter 12.

[3] Richard Littledale, *Stale Bread: A Handbook for Speaking the Story* (Edinburgh: Saint Andrew Press 2011), p. 46.

[4] Thomas H. Troeger, *Imagining a Sermon* (Nashville, TN: Abingdon Press, 1990), p. 113.

7

www.ingramcontent.com/pod-product-compliance
Lightning Source LLC
Chambersburg PA
CBHW070048100426
42734CB00040B/2757